HOW GOD SPEAKS

Hearing, Recognizing and
Understanding the Voice of God

By

Rev. Dr. David Okumgba

First Paperback Edition 2025

ISBN:

Rev. Dr. David Okumgba

P. O. Box 1492,

Alief, TX 77411

All Scripture quoted from NIV and NKJV (copyright 1994 by Thomas Nelson, Inc.) versions of the Bibles

PRINTED IN THE UNITED STATES OF AMERICA

Table of Contents

INTRODUCTION

How God Speaks: Hearing, Recognizing, and Understanding the Voice of God

God is a speaking God. From the very beginning, creation itself was born by His voice: *"And God said…"* (Genesis 1:3). His voice carries power, wisdom, and purpose—and it is through His voice that we come to understand His will, walk in His ways, and fulfill our divine assignment on earth.

Yet, despite God's willingness to speak, many struggle to recognize when He is speaking. **Job 33:14** captures this dilemma succinctly: *"For God may speak in one way, or in another, yet man does not perceive it."* The problem is not that God is silent; the problem is spiritual perception. God is always speaking—whether through Scripture, the Holy Spirit, dreams, visions, circumstances, or even a still small voice—but we must learn to hear, discern, and respond.

Success in Life Begins with Hearing God

To succeed in life, you must know God's will. To know His will, you must recognize His voice. **Ephesians 5:17** exhorts us, *"Therefore do not be unwise, but understand what the will of the Lord is."* Wisdom begins with the ability to hear God, and that hearing requires more than casual acquaintance; it demands relationship.

Just as Elijah discovered in **1 Kings 19:11-12**, God's voice is not always in the wind, fire, or earthquake—it may come as a gentle whisper. This teaches us that God is not bound by method. He speaks in diverse ways at different times, and we must not limit Him to one particular mode of communication. Our sensitivity to His voice will determine how accurately we follow His direction.

Developing Spiritual Sensitivity

Spiritual sensitivity is developed through **fellowship with God**—through prayer, the study of His Word, worship, and engaging in Christian community. As we draw closer to Him, His voice becomes clearer. Just as a child easily recognizes the voice of a parent in a crowd, so can we grow to hear God with clarity and confidence.

God wants you to hear Him. He longs for fellowship with His children and desires to guide you daily. Jesus said in **John 10:27**, *"My sheep hear My voice, and I know them, and they follow Me."* This book is written to help you become one of those who confidently hears and follows the Shepherd's voice.

In This Book, You Will Discover:

1. **The Many Ways God Speaks**
   Through Scripture, the Holy Spirit, godly counsel, spiritual impressions, circumstances, worship, dreams, visions, and even silence.
2. **How to Develop Spiritual Sensitivity**
   So you can discern God's voice amidst life's noise and distractions. Recognizing His voice is a spiritual skill that must be cultivated.
3. **The Foundational Role of Scripture**
   God's Word is the ultimate standard for all divine communication. **Hebrews 1:1-2** declares that *"God, who at various times and in various ways spoke in time past to the fathers by the prophets, has in these last days spoken to us by His Son…"* His Word is eternal. **Mark 13:31** reminds us, *"Heaven and earth will pass away, but My words will by no means pass away."*
4. **The Power of Fellowship with God**
   Deepening your relationship with God through **prayer, meditation**, and **fellowship with believers** sharpens your hearing and empowers your walk.
5. **Faith and Confidence to Follow Divine Guidance**
   As you grow in hearing God, your faith to obey and overcome increases. **1 John 5:4** assures us, *"For whatever is born of God overcomes the world. And this is the victory that has overcome the world — our faith."*

It's Not About Volume—It's About Relationship

Hearing God is not a mystical experience reserved for a select few; it is the **inheritance of every believer**. It is not about volume or dramatic encounters—it is about relationship. The closer you walk with God, the more familiar His voice becomes. And when you are tuned to His frequency, **divine direction becomes a lifestyle**, not a rare event.

Are You Ready to Hear God Clearly?

By the time you finish this book, you will not only understand **how God speaks,** but you will be equipped to **recognize His voice, respond with confidence**, and **walk in divine purpose**. Your journey to hearing God more clearly begins now.

Let's begin.

Chapter 1

Why It Is Vital to Know the Voice of God

John 10:27
My sheep hear My voice, and I know them, and they follow Me.

The first and most critical question we want to answer is this: **Why is it vital to know or recognize the voice of God?**

1. To Understand His Will

Ephesians 5:17
Therefore do not be unwise but understand what the will of the Lord is.

The will of God is essential for living a victorious, fulfilled life and securing eternal life.

The Voice of God Reveals His Will

Jeremiah 7:23
But this is what I commanded them, saying, 'Obey My voice, and I will be your God, and you shall be My people.

And walk in all the ways that I have commanded you, that it may be well with you.'

We understand God's will for our lives by hearing what He says to us. His voice communicates His desire, purpose, and direction for our lives.

Three Types of Will at Work in the World

Self-Will – The Will of Man

Self-will is the desire of man to live apart from God, to make choices independent of His guidance. God warned against this in His Word.

Jeremiah 10:23

O Lord, I know the way of man is not in himself; It is not in man who walks to direct his own steps.

Man does not have the capacity to direct himself. He was created to be led by God.

Proverbs 14:12

There is a way that seems right to a man, But its end is the way of death.

Self-will operates through the flesh. To walk in self-will is to walk in the flesh.

Romans 8:1

There is therefore now no condemnation to those who are in

Christ Jesus, who do not walk according to the flesh, but according to the Spirit.

2 Peter 2:10
and especially those who walk according to the flesh in the lust of uncleanness and despise authority. They are presumptuous, self-willed. They are not afraid to speak evil of dignitaries.

The result of self-will is abandonment by God.

Psalm 81:11-12
"But My people would not heed My voice, And Israel would have none of Me. 12 So I gave them over to their own stubborn heart, To walk in their own counsels."

Sin, suffering, and trouble in the world are largely due to man's self-will. David spoke of self-will operating in the lives of wicked people.

Psalm 27:12
Do not deliver me to the will of my adversaries; For false witnesses have risen against me, And such as breathe out violence.

Satan's Will
Satan has a will, and his will is to destroy. His mission is to rob you of God's blessings and take you to hell.

John 10:10
The thief does not come except to steal, and to kill, and to

It Determines Your Eternal Destiny

Your eternal destiny depends on doing the will of God. You must respond positively to His plan of redemption.

Matthew 7:21
"Not everyone who says to Me, 'Lord, Lord,' shall enter the kingdom of heaven, but he who does the will of My Father in heaven."

1 John 2:17
And the world is passing away, and the lust of it; but he who does the will of God abides forever.

It Is the Basis of Your Relationship with God

Doing God's will defines your relationship with Him.

Mark 3:35
For whoever does the will of God is My brother and My sister and mother."

It Provides Direction for Life

You do not have the ability to guide your own steps. Without God's will and direction, you stray from His purpose.

Jeremiah 10:23
O Lord, I know the way of man is not in himself; It is not in man who walks to direct his own steps.

Isaiah 53:6
All we like sheep have gone astray; We have turned, every

one, to his own way; And the Lord has laid on Him the iniquity of us all.

It Gives Knowledge of the Future
God alone knows the future. He knows the traps of Satan, the state of nations, and what lies ahead for you.

Isaiah 46:10
Declaring the end from the beginning, And from ancient times things that are not yet done, Saying, 'My counsel shall stand, And I will do all My pleasure.'

Man can only live in the present, recall the past, and plan for the future. Only God has full knowledge of what will actually happen.

Some people mistakenly think Satan knows the future. He does not. If he had known, he would not have incited the crucifixion of Jesus, which led to mankind's redemption. Satan only knows what God reveals.

It Is a Divine Command
You are commanded to know and obey the will of God.

Ephesians 5:17
Therefore do not be unwise, but understand what the will of the Lord is.

Ephesians 6:6
not with eyeservice, as men-pleasers, but as bondservants of Christ, doing the will of God from the heart.

God values obedience to His will more than religious rituals or sacrifices.

1 Samuel 15:22
So Samuel said: "Has the Lord as great delight in burnt offerings and sacrifices, As in obeying the voice of the Lord? Behold, to obey is better than sacrifice, And to heed than the fat of rams."

God desires that you stand perfect and complete in His will.

Colossians 4:12
Epaphras, who is one of you, a bondservant of Christ, greets you, always laboring fervently for you in prayers, that you may stand perfect and complete in all the will of God.

It Produces Spiritual Maturity and Doctrinal Soundness
If you obey the will of God as revealed to you, you will grow spiritually and avoid doctrinal error.

John 7:17
If anyone wills to do His will, he shall know concerning the doctrine, whether it is from God or whether I speak on My own authority.

It Gets Your Prayers Answered
When you live in the will of God, you can pray with confidence and expect answers.

1 John 3:22
And whatever we ask we receive from Him, because we keep His commandments and do those things that are pleasing in His sight.

1 John 5:14-15
Now this is the confidence that we have in Him, that if we ask anything according to His will, He hears us. 15 And if we know that He hears us, whatever we ask, we know that we have the petitions that we have asked of Him.

John 9:31
Now we know that God does not hear sinners; but if anyone is a worshiper of God and does His will, He hears him.

It Guarantees the Fulfillment of God's Promises and Blessings

When you obey God's will, His promises will be fulfilled in your life, and His blessings will overtake you.

Hebrews 10:36
For you have need of endurance, so that after you have done the will of God, you may receive the promise.

Deuteronomy 28:1-2
"Now it shall come to pass, if you diligently obey the voice of the Lord your God, to observe carefully all His commandments which I command you today, that the Lord your God will set you high above all nations of the earth. 2 And all these blessings shall come upon you and overtake you, because you obey the voice of the Lord your God:"

It Guarantees Prosperity and Good Success

Joshua 1:8
This Book of the Law shall not depart from your mouth, but you shall meditate in it day and night, that you may observe to do according to all that is written in it. For then you will make your way prosperous, and then you will have good success.

It Secures the Presence of God
God's presence remains with those who do His will.

John 8:29
And He who sent Me is with Me. The Father has not left Me alone, for I always do those things that please Him."

Knowing and doing the will of God is the **secret to a victorious, prosperous, and fulfilled life**.

2. To Avoid Being Deceived by Other Voices

Many people have fallen into the trap of deception because they listened to voices they believed were from God, but were not. One of the clearest examples of this is found in the story of the young prophet and the old prophet during the reign of King Jeroboam.

The Young Prophet's Tragedy — 1 Kings 13:1-32

In 1 Kings 13, a young prophet was sent by God to prophesy against the altar built by King Jeroboam at Bethel. The prophet obeyed God's instruction, delivered the prophecy, and rejected the king's offer to eat and drink in the city—because God had clearly commanded him **not to eat or drink there**.

However, on his way out of the city, an old prophet met him and lied to him. The old prophet claimed an angel had instructed him to bring the young prophet back to his house to eat and drink. Believing the lie, the young prophet disobeyed God's original command and went with the old prophet.

As a result of this disobedience, the young prophet was killed by a lion when he left the old prophet's house. His death was a direct consequence of listening to a **deceptive voice** rather than obeying the **voice of God**.

The Voice of God Protects from Deception

John 10:4-5
And when he brings out his own sheep, he goes before them; and the sheep follow him, for they know his voice. 5 Yet they will by no means follow a stranger, but will flee from him, for they do not know the voice of strangers."

When you know the voice of God, you will not follow a stranger's voice. You will be able to discern deception and avoid it.

Many Voices Are Speaking in the World Today

1 Corinthians 14:10 (KJV)
There are, it may be, so many kinds of voices in the world, and none of them is without signification.

Every voice you hear has meaning and influence, but **not all voices are from God**. Discernment is needed.

Types of Voices You Must Recognize

The Voice of Man
This is the audible voice of people — parents, spouses, children, friends, teachers, pastors, mentors, and authority figures. These voices can have a lasting impact on our lives. Some of us still hear the influence of words spoken over us years ago.

However, **when the voice of man contradicts the voice or Word of God**, you must choose to obey God.

Acts 5:29
But Peter and the other apostles answered and said: "We ought to obey God rather than men."

The Voice of Satan
The first time Satan's voice was heard was in the Garden of Eden when he deceived Eve.

Genesis 3:1, 4-5
Satan twisted God's Word to lead Eve into sin. His voice **always seeks to deceive, lie, and lead people away from God's purpose**.

Satan's voice sometimes comes **through people**, as it did through Peter when he tried to stop Jesus from going to the cross.

Matthew 16:21-23
From that time Jesus began to show to His disciples that He must go to Jerusalem, and suffer many things... 22 Then Peter took Him aside and began to rebuke Him, saying, "Far be it from You, Lord; this shall not happen to You!" 23 But He turned and said to Peter, "Get behind Me, Satan! You are an offense to Me, for you are not mindful of the things of God, but the things of men."

Satan's voice is often **disguised behind well-meaning people**, but the intention is always to lead you away from God's will.

False prophets today often speak **with Satan's voice** under the guise of religious prophecy. Their words promote **fear, guilt, bondage, and deception**, not freedom.

Satan's voice can also come **through demon spirits** using the vocal cords of human beings.

Mark 1:23-24
Now there was a man in their synagogue with an unclean spirit. And he cried out, 24 saying, "Let us alone! What have we to do with You, Jesus of Nazareth? Did You come to destroy us? I know who You are — the Holy One of God!"

Sometimes, demons speak audibly through possessed people, but **most often, Satan speaks inaudibly** — injecting **thoughts** that contradict God's will.

The Voice of Self
This is when you talk to yourself or think within yourself.

Luke 16:3
"Then the steward said within himself, 'What shall I do? For my master is taking the stewardship away from me. I cannot dig; I am ashamed to beg.'"

Luke 15:17-19
"But when he came to himself, he said, 'How many of my father's hired servants have bread enough and to spare, and I perish with hunger! 18 I will arise and go to my father, and will say to him, "Father, I have sinned against heaven and before you, 19 and I am no longer worthy to be called your son. Make me like one of your hired servants."'"

The voice of self is **unreliable** unless it reflects **God's voice and Word**. Many times, it aligns with **fleshly desires or Satan's influence**.

The Voice of God
Jesus said His sheep **can know His voice** and distinguish it from others.

John 10:4-5
And when he brings out his own sheep, he goes before them; and the sheep follow him, for they know his voice. 5 Yet they will by no means follow a stranger, but will flee from him, for they do not know the voice of strangers."

Knowing God's voice empowers you to **avoid deception, resist error**, and **walk in His perfect will**.

3. The Power of God is Released Through His Voice

The voice of God is not just a method of communication; it is a **channel of supernatural power**. Whenever God speaks, **power is released** to accomplish His will.

The Power of God's Voice in Scripture

Psalm 29:3-5
The voice of the Lord is over the waters; The God of glory thunders; The Lord is over many waters. 4 The voice of the Lord is powerful; The voice of the Lord is full of majesty. 5

The voice of the Lord breaks the cedars, Yes, the Lord splinters the cedars of Lebanon.

Isaiah 30:31
For through the voice of the Lord Assyria will be beaten down, As He strikes with the rod.

Psalm 46:6
The nations raged, the kingdoms were moved; He uttered His voice, the earth melted.

Psalm 18:13
The Lord thundered from heaven, And the Most High uttered His voice, Hailstones and coals of fire.

Psalm 29:7-9
The voice of the Lord divides the flames of fire. 8 The voice of the Lord shakes the wilderness; The Lord shakes the Wilderness of Kadesh. 9 The voice of the Lord makes the deer give birth, And strips the forests bare; And in His temple everyone says, "Glory!"

God's voice causes mountains to move, nations to tremble, and nature to respond. **His voice changes everything**.

The Word of God Must Become the Voice of God in Your Life

Until the **Word of God becomes the voice of God** in your life, it cannot transform you. The Word must come alive in your heart and be declared through your mouth.

Joshua 1:8
8 This Book of the Law shall not depart from your mouth, but you shall meditate in it day and night, that you may observe to do according to all that is written in it. For then you will make your way prosperous, and then you will have good success.

Logos and Rhema: The Written Word and the Living Voice

In the Bible, two Greek words are translated as *"word"*: **logos** and **rhema**.

- **Logos** – the *written* Word of God, the Scriptures.
- **Rhema** – the *spoken*, life-giving, specific Word of God—His voice to you in a given moment.

The *logos* is God's Word in written form; the *rhema* is God's Word made alive and personal by His Spirit. **Power is not released until the *logos* becomes *rhema* in your life**—until the written Word comes alive in your heart as God's personal voice to you.

John 6:63
It is the Spirit who gives life; the flesh profits nothing. The words that I speak to you are spirit, and they are life.

The *logos* brings knowledge; the *rhema* brings revelation for a specific situation. Peter did not walk on water simply by knowing the *logos*—he acted on a *rhema*. He asked Jesus for a specific word, and Jesus said, *"Come."* That was a word for Peter alone, not for the others in the boat. Faith responded to the *rhema*, and Peter walked on water.

Matthew 4:4
It is written, "Man shall not live by bread alone, but by every word that proceeds from the mouth of God."

This means we do not live merely by what was written long ago, but by the *rhema*—the word currently proceeding from God's mouth into our lives. Transformation, healing, deliverance, and breakthrough come when the written Word becomes the spoken Word to you now.

How the Logos Becomes Rhema

The process is revealed in:

Hebrews 4:2
For indeed the gospel was preached to us as well as to them; but the word which they heard did not profit them, not being mixed with faith in those who heard it.

When the written Word (*logos*) is **mixed with faith**, it becomes *rhema*. Faith takes the Word from the page into your heart and then out of your mouth as the living voice of God.

Without the written Word, you cannot have the voice of God. Without the voice of God, there is no transformation. The voice of God will never contradict the written Word. That's how you recognize it — it always agrees with Scripture.

Knowing God's voice begins with knowing God's Word.

The Voice of God Over the Word of God

Psalm 29:3
The voice of the Lord is over the waters; the God of glory thunders.

In **Ephesians 5:26,** *water* is symbolic of the Word of God:

That He might sanctify and cleanse her with the washing of water by the word.

Psalm 29:3 is telling us — the voice of the Lord flows over the Word. As you **read, hear, study, memorize, and meditate** on Scripture, the voice of God will rise within your spirit, releasing the power to accomplish what you've read or heard — in the name of Jesus.

Summary: Why It Is Vital to Know the Voice of God

1. **To understand His will** — for direction, destiny, and blessing.
2. **To avoid deception** — and escape misleading voices.
3. **Because His power is released through His voice** — to change your life and circumstances.

Prayers

Prayer 1
Father, in the name of Jesus, let everything hindering me and every reader from hearing Your voice and knowing Your individual will be **consumed by fire** and flushed out of our lives today. Open our ears and hearts to know Your voice and respond in obedience, in Jesus' name. *(Proverbs 4:20)*

Prayer 2
Father, in the name of Jesus, by the witness of the Holy Spirit and the realignment of our spiritual ears, help me and every reader to recognize Your voice. Empower us to understand Your will, escape deception, and access the **power in Your voice** for a change of story, in Jesus' name. *(Ephesians 5:17; John 10:4-5; Psalm 29:3-5)*

Chapter 2

Four Questions You Must Answer

Jeremiah 29:13
And you will seek Me and find Me, when you search for Me with all your heart.

We serve a God who hides Himself. Therefore, to hear His voice, we must seek Him with all our hearts.

Isaiah 45:15
Truly You are God, who hide Yourself, O God of Israel, the Savior!

Before we can position ourselves to hear from God, there are **four critical questions** we must honestly answer.

Question 1: Do You Really Want to Hear God's Voice?

Not everyone truly desires to hear God for themselves.

Some prefer a middleman.
When God spoke to Israel at Mount Sinai, the people were so overwhelmed by His voice that they begged Moses to act as a go-between:

Deuteronomy 5:23–27

"So it was, when you heard the voice from the midst of the darkness, while the mountain was burning with fire, that you came near to me, all the heads of your tribes and your elders. 24 And you said: 'Surely the Lord our God has shown us His glory and His greatness, and we have heard His voice from the midst of the fire. We have seen this day that God speaks with man; yet he still lives. 25 Now therefore, why should we die? For this great fire will consume us; if we hear the voice of the Lord our God anymore, then we shall die. 26 For who is there of all flesh who has heard the voice of the living God speaking from the midst of the fire, as we have, and lived? 27 You go near and hear all that the Lord our God may say, and tell us all that the Lord our God says to you, and we will hear and do it.'

They feared that hearing God directly might cost them their lives — so they asked Moses to hear from God and relay the message.

Some avoid God's voice out of fear.
Others resist hearing from God because they worry He might ask them to do something they don't want to do, or make demands they feel unprepared to meet. At the root, this is a **trust issue** — a lack of confidence in God's will and goodness.

Here's the truth for those in this category:

1. **God never commands without enabling.**
   Whatever He tells you to do, He will empower you to accomplish.

2. **God's requests are for your benefit, not His.** He doesn't need your resources—His instructions are always for your blessing and reward.

   Isaiah 45:19
   "I have not spoken in secret, in a dark place of the earth; I did not say to the seed of Jacob, 'Seek Me in vain'…"

3. **God's plan for your life always surpasses your own.**

   Proverbs 4:18
   "The path of the just is like the shining sun, that shines ever brighter unto the perfect day."

Are you willing to pay the price?

Hearing God's voice comes with a cost—not in money, but in discipline:

- **Patience** – waiting on Him without rushing the process.
- **Focus** – guarding your mind from distractions.
- **Diligence** – seeking Him earnestly and consistently.
- **Submission** – yielding to His will, even before you know all the details.

Habakkuk 2:1
"I will stand my watch and set myself on the rampart, and

watch to see what He will say to me, and what I will answer when I am corrected."

Question 2: Why Do You Want to Hear the Voice of God?

The next question we must confront is about **motivation**. Everything with God begins and ends with the heart's intent.

Pure motives attract God's favor.
Solomon asked for wisdom—not for personal gain, but so he could serve God and His people more effectively. That selfless request pleased God, and He blessed Solomon abundantly.

1 Kings 3:9
"Therefore give to Your servant an understanding heart to judge Your people, that I may discern between good and evil..."

Selfish motives repel God's power.
Simon the sorcerer tried to buy the power of the Holy Spirit to manipulate and control people. Peter's response was swift and severe.

Acts 8:18–23
"Your money perish with you, because you thought that the gift of God could be purchased with money!"

In essence, we could reframe this question: **Do you truly want to know God's will — or do you only want His voice to confirm your own desires?**

Jesus made it clear: life is not sustained by material needs alone but by every word that proceeds from the mouth of God. A genuine hunger for His will is what positions you to hear His voice.

David modeled this posture. His deepest longing was to dwell in God's presence and receive His direction before making any move:

Psalm 27:4
"One thing I have desired of the Lord, that will I seek: that I may dwell in the house of the Lord all the days of my life, to behold the beauty of the Lord, and to inquire in His temple."

When you become desperate — not just for answers, but for **God's will above your own** — you are ready to hear His voice.

Question 3: Are You Ready to Do His Will?

Your readiness to obey is one of the most important qualifications for hearing God's voice. Jesus made this clear when He said:

John 7:17
"If anyone wills to do His will, he shall know concerning the doctrine, whether it is from God or whether I speak on My own authority."

In other words, the person whose heart is already inclined toward obedience will be able to recognize God's voice and discern His truth. The opposite is also true: if you are not prepared to submit to what God says, His voice will remain distant or unclear.

The rich young ruler in **Matthew 19:16–22** is a striking example. He came to Jesus seeking eternal life, but when Jesus told him to sell his possessions, give to the poor, and follow Him, he went away sorrowful. He could not surrender to God's will in that area of his life. What he failed to realize was the promise in **Proverbs 19:17**: *"He who has pity on the poor lends to the Lord, and He will pay back what he has given."* Had he obeyed, the outcome would have been far greater than the sacrifice.

God does not speak simply for the sake of speaking. His words are always purposeful and often carry instructions that require a response. Those who consistently obey the light they already have will find that God continues to speak, guiding them step by step. Conversely, ignoring or resisting His known will can close the door to further direction.

Obedience to the written Word is the clearest evidence of a heart ready to receive the spoken Word. If the truth you already know has not been acted upon, you cannot expect fresh guidance. God's leading is progressive—each step builds on the one before it. Until the last instruction is followed, the next one will not come.

Hearing His voice, therefore, is not merely about listening; it is about living in such a way that when God speaks, you are already prepared to say, "Yes, Lord."

Question 4: What Kind of Listener Are You?

In **Matthew 13:18-23**, Jesus identifies **four types of listeners**—four kinds of hearts.

Matthew 13:18-23
"Therefore hear the parable of the sower: 19 When anyone hears the word of the kingdom, and does not understand it, then the wicked one comes and snatches away what was sown in his heart. This is he who received seed by the wayside. 20 But he who received the seed on stony places, this is he who hears the word and immediately receives it with joy; 21 yet he has no root in himself, but endures only for a while. For when tribulation or persecution arises because of the word, immediately he stumbles.
22 Now he who received seed among the thorns is he who hears the word, and the cares of this world and the

deceitfulness of riches choke the word, and he becomes unfruitful. 23 But he who received seed on the good ground is he who hears the word and understands it, who indeed bears fruit and produces: some a hundredfold, some sixty, some thirty."

The Closed Listener (Wayside)

Matthew 13:19
When anyone hears the word of the kingdom, and does not understand it, then the wicked one comes and snatches away what was sown in his heart. This is he who received seed by the wayside.

- The **wayside** is ground hardened by heavy traffic.
- These are people **hardened by life's experiences**, sin, busyness, or false beliefs.
- Their hearts are closed to God's word — unresponsive and resistant.
- They may have **prejudged the word**, the messenger, or the message.
- Fear, pride, and self-centeredness **rule their hearts** and lock out God.
- The Word is **snatched away by the devil** before it can take root.

The Shallow Listener (Stony Places)

Matthew 13:20-21
But he who received the seed on stony places, this is he who hears the word and immediately receives it with joy; 21 yet

he has no root in himself, but endures only for a while. For when tribulation or persecution arises because of the word, immediately he stumbles.

- These are **superficial listeners**, emotional but not transformed.
- They receive the Word with joy but **lack depth or root**.
- Their motives are often **selfish or misguided**.
- When **trials or delays** arise, they abandon the Word.
- **Simon the Sorcerer** (Acts 8:9-24) is an example — initially joyful, but not truly changed.

The Carnal or Distracted Listener (Among Thorns)

Matthew 13:22
Now he who received seed among the thorns is he who hears the word, and the cares of this world and the deceitfulness of riches choke the word, and he becomes unfruitful.

- These are **worldly, divided, and distracted listeners**.
- They are **preoccupied with life's cares** — money, fame, fashion, success.
- They attend church, but **bear no spiritual fruit**.
- Their focus on **worldly gain** chokes the Word's effectiveness.

- **Ananias and Sapphira** (Acts 5:1-11) represent this category—more concerned with image and possessions than with God.

The Good Listener (Good Ground)

Matthew 13:23
But he who received seed on the good ground is he who hears the word and understands it, who indeed bears fruit and produces: some a hundredfold, some sixty, some thirty."

- These listeners **receive, understand, and apply** the Word.
- They bear **visible, lasting fruit**.
- **Cornelius** (Acts 10:1-48) and the **Ethiopian Eunuch** (Acts 8:26-40) are examples.
- The **depth of their understanding** determines their fruitfulness.

Note: You May Not Be One Type All the Time

- You might be **receptive in some areas** and **closed in others**.
- Open to **prayer**, but closed to **giving** or **evangelism**.
- The **evidence of hearing God's voice** in any area is **fruitfulness** in that area.

Prayer 1

Father, in the name of Jesus, tune every reader to Your frequency. Line me and every reader up with Your Word and Your thoughts. Enhance our spiritual antenna and receptors. Silence every noise and contrary voice. Destroy every carnality. Open my ears and the ears of every reader to hear Your voice continually, in the name of Jesus. *(Ephesians 1:17-18; Psalm 119:18)*

Prayer 2

Father, in the name of Jesus, I offer my body as a living sacrifice unto You. My body is Your temple. Move in me, talk in me, walk in me. Take all of me. Let everything resisting my total submission and surrender to Your will be crucified today. Empower my transformation through the continuous renewal of my mind so that my spiritual senses will become matured enough to discern Your voice and Your will. Do the same for every reader, in the name of Jesus. *(Romans 12:1-2; Hebrews 5:13-14)*

Chapter 3

Precondition for Knowing the Voice of God

A precondition is a prerequisite for qualifying or reaching a particular goal.

John 10:2-5
But he who enters by the door is the shepherd of the sheep. 3 To him the doorkeeper opens, and the sheep hear his voice; and he calls his own sheep by name and leads them out. 4 And when he brings out his own sheep, he goes before them; and the sheep follow him, for they know his voice. 5 Yet they will by no means follow a stranger, but will flee from him, for they do not know the voice of strangers."

Preconditions to Knowing the Voice of the Lord

1. You Must Be Born Again

John 10:27
My sheep hear My voice, and I know them, and they follow Me.

To hear God's voice, you must be His sheep. You must belong to Christ to be familiar with His voice and recognize it. Just as in the natural realm we recognize the voices of those we know, in the spiritual realm, familiarity with God's voice begins with relationship.

Does God speak to unbelievers? Yes, usually through dreams and visions, but they often need a believer to help them understand.

- **Pharaoh** heard God through a dream but needed **Joseph** to interpret it. **Genesis 41:1-33**
- **Nebuchadnezzar** also received a dream from God but needed **Daniel** to interpret it. **Daniel 2:1-45**
- **Cornelius** in **Acts 10:1-34** received a vision and was told to send for **Peter**.

Even Jesus spoke to **unbelievers in parables** to hide the mysteries of the kingdom.

Matthew 13:10-11
And the disciples came and said to Him, "Why do You speak to them in parables?" 11 He answered and said to them, "Because it has been given to you to know the mysteries of the kingdom of heaven, but to them it has not been given."

Jesus told Nicodemus that unless one is born again he cannot understand the kingdom of God.

John 3:3
Jesus answered and said to him, "Most assuredly, I say to

you, unless one is born again, he cannot see the kingdom of God."

Many of us heard God speak to us even during our days of unbelief, often through dreams and visions. However, at the time, we didn't truly understand or value His voice. When God speaks to unbelievers, He often leads them externally — through circumstances, dreams, and visions or supernatural encounters. But once we become believers, His leading shifts inward, through the indwelling presence of the Holy Spirit.

2. You Must Be Baptized in the Holy Spirit

Acts 1:8
But you shall receive power when the Holy Spirit has come upon you; and you shall be witnesses to Me in Jerusalem, and in all Judea and Samaria, and to the end of the earth."

This baptism is separate from salvation. It enables the Holy Spirit to dwell within and lead from inside.

John 14:15-17
"If you love Me, keep My commandments. 16 And I will pray the Father, and He will give you another Helper, that He may abide with you forever — 17 the Spirit of truth, whom the world cannot receive, because it neither sees Him nor knows Him; but you know Him, for He dwells with you and will be in you."

The Holy Spirit guides believers into God's will:

John 16:13-14
However, when He, the Spirit of truth, has come, He will guide you into all truth; for He will not speak on His own authority, but whatever He hears He will speak; and He will tell you things to come. 14 He will glorify Me, for He will take of what is Mine and declare it to you."

How the Holy Spirit Helps You Know God's Voice:

- **Empowers you to overcome sin,** and live righteously so that you are not disconnected from the voice of God.

  Isaiah 59:2
  But your iniquities have separated you from your God; And your sins have hidden His face from you, So that He will not hear.

- **Empowers you to walk in the Spirit** so that you will be sensitive to the voice of God.

  Revelation 1:10
  I was in the Spirit on the Lord's Day, and I heard behind me a loud voice, as of a trumpet,

  The reason John heard the voice of God was because he was in the spirit. The Holy Spirit empowers you to be in the spirit.

Galatians 5:16
I say then: Walk in the Spirit, and you shall not fulfill the lust of the flesh.

Walking in the spirit keeps you tuned into the frequency of God to hear his voice.

- **Helps you pray effectively** and prayer is communication with God.

Romans 8:26-27
Likewise the Spirit also helps in our weaknesses. For we do not know what we should pray for as we ought, but the Spirit Himself makes intercession for us with groanings which cannot be uttered. 27 Now He who searches the hearts knows what the mind of the Spirit is, because He makes intercession for the saints according to the will of God.

- **Bears witness to confirm God's voice**:

Romans 8:16
The Spirit Himself bears witness with our spirit that we are children of God,

- **Operates the gifts of the Spirit** which enhances our communication with God

1 Corinthians 12:4-11
There are [a]diversities of gifts, but the same Spirit. 5 There are differences of ministries, but the same Lord. 6 And there are diversities of activities, but it is

the same God who works [b]all in all. 7 But the manifestation of the Spirit is given to each one for the profit of all: 8 for to one is given the word of wisdom through the Spirit, to another the word of knowledge through the same Spirit, 9 to another faith by the same Spirit, to another gifts of healings by [c]the same Spirit, 10 to another the working of miracles, to another prophecy, to another discerning of spirits, to another different kinds of tongues, to another the interpretation of tongues. 11 But one and the same Spirit works all these things, distributing to each one individually as He wills.

To truly recognize God's voice, the Holy Spirit must dwell in you.

3. You Must Be Spiritual - to access and understand spiritual things.

1 Corinthians 2:14
But the natural man does not receive the things of the Spirit of God, for they are foolishness to him; nor can he know them, because they are spiritually discerned.

Being born again is not the same as being spiritual. The **Corinthians** were born again but **carnal**. Salvation doesn't automatically make you spiritual—it simply initiates you into the realm of the Spirit. Being born again is your entry point, not your end point. If you're truly interested in spiritual growth, you must intentionally pursue and develop the new spiritual nature you've received.

1 Corinthians 3:3
for you are still carnal. For where there are envy, strife, and divisions among you, are you not carnal and behaving like mere men?

To be carnal is to be consumed and ruled by the flesh. To let the flesh determine all your choices and decisions. It is the opposite of spirituality

Romans 8:5-6
For those who live according to the flesh set their minds on the things of the flesh, but those who live according to the Spirit, the things of the Spirit. 6 For to be carnally minded is death, but to be spiritually minded is life and peace."

What It Means to Be Spiritual:

- **Under the Holy Spirit's control**: To be spiritual means living under the constant influence of the Holy Spirit, who operates through your human spirit. At every moment, you are either being controlled by the Spirit or by the flesh — there is no neutral ground. You are "in the Spirit" only to the degree that the Spirit is in control of you. When Apostle John heard the voice of Jesus, it was because he was fully yielded to the Spirit's influence

Revelation 1:10
I was in the Spirit on the Lord's Day, and I heard behind me a loud voice, as of a trumpet,

- **Led by the Spirit of God**:

Romans 8:14
For as many as are led by the Spirit of God, these are sons of God.

- **Mind ruled by God's Word**:

John 15:7
If you abide in Me, and My words abide in you, you will ask what you desire, and it shall be done for you.

Colossians 3:2
Set your mind on things above, not on things on the earth.

- **Praying in tongues**:

1 Corinthians 14:14
For if I pray in a tongue, my spirit prays, but my understanding is unfruitful.

According to James 3:1–5, whatever controls the tongue ultimately controls the whole body. So when I pray in tongues, my tongue is being directed by my spirit—which, in turn, is submitted to the Spirit of God. That means my entire being comes under spiritual authority in that moment, making me truly spiritual at that point in time.

1 Corinthians 14:2
For he who speaks in a tongue does not speak to men but to God, for no one understands him; however, in the spirit he speaks mysteries.

This means that praying in tongues ushers me into the realm of the Spirit, where I engage with divine mysteries. In that moment, I am operating in the Spirit—fully spiritual and aligned with the purposes of God.

4. You Must Be Submitted and Surrendered to His Will

Romans 12:1-2
I beseech you therefore, brethren, by the mercies of God, that you present your bodies a living sacrifice, holy, acceptable to God, which is your reasonable service. 2 And do not be conformed to this world, but be transformed by the renewing of your mind, that you may prove what is that good and acceptable and perfect will of God.

In the Old Testament, when a sacrifice was offered to God, it was usually **completely burned**. The sacrifice had **no claims to its life**. A **living sacrifice** refers to a life **totally surrendered** to God, not living for itself, but fully for Him.

Many people want to know God's will **before deciding** if they will submit to it. But that's **reversing the order**. God expects you to be **surrendered first** before He reveals His will to you. Your **submission precedes revelation**.

Evidence of Surrender

Your attitude to the **written will of God** shows the depth of your surrender. The way you respond to **scriptural commands** like:

- Give thanks in everything
- Fear not
- Study the Word
- Seek first the Kingdom of God
- Love your neighbor
- Serve one another
- Pray, give, and preach the Gospel

These reveal how **surrendered you truly are**. Your **obedience to these commands** determines your **capacity to hear and recognize God's voice**.

What Does It Mean to Surrender?

- You give up **your right to yourself**
- You give up **your right to be angry or retaliate**
- You give up **your ambitions, time, money, and reputation**

- You give up **your relationships and your very life**
- You even give up **your right to determine the outcome of your obedience**

True success is **knowing God's will and obeying it, regardless of the outcome**.

Paul's Example of Surrender

Paul was warned that **chains and tribulation** awaited him in Jerusalem, yet he was undeterred because he was **surrendered** to God's will.

Acts 20:22-24
And see, now I go bound in the spirit to Jerusalem, not knowing the things that will happen to me there, 23 except that the Holy Spirit testifies in every city, saying that chains and tribulations await me. 24 But none of these things move me; nor do I count my life dear to myself, so that I may finish my race with joy, and the ministry which I received from the Lord Jesus, to testify to the gospel of the grace of God.

Paul was **not concerned about his safety**; he had already given up his right to the outcome of obedience. This is the essence of surrender.

Why People Hesitate to Surrender

True submission means yielding fully to God's will. If you want to hear and recognize His voice, surrender must come first. Many struggle with surrender because they don't truly understand that God's will is always good, acceptable, and perfect. We hesitate to let go because we haven't fully grasped this foundational truth: God's plan for our lives far exceeds anything we could ever imagine for ourselves.

Jeremiah 29:11 (NIV)
"For I know the plans I have for you," declares the Lord, "plans to prosper you and not to harm you, plans to give you hope and a future."

God's plan is **far better than any plan** you could make for yourself.

5. Your Mind Must Be Renewed Continuously

Romans 12:2
And do not be conformed to this world, but be transformed by the renewing of your mind, that you may prove what is that good and acceptable and perfect will of God.

The **unrenewed mind** is the **greatest hindrance** to hearing God's voice. It is naturally **conformed to worldly principles**, dominated by the flesh, and **in constant conflict with the Spirit**.

Galatians 5:16-17
I say then: Walk in the Spirit, and you shall not fulfill the lust of the flesh. 17 For the flesh lusts against the Spirit, and

the Spirit against the flesh; and these are contrary to one another, so that you do not do the things that you wish.

Every blessing God has for you is already **released into your spirit,** but your **unrenewed mind blocks its manifestation.**

Ephesians 1:3
(Paraphrased) Every spiritual blessing is already yours, but it is accessed through a **renewed mind.**

Any area where your mind is **not renewed** is an area where you will **struggle to hear God's voice.** This is why some believers can hear God clearly in certain areas of their lives while remaining completely deaf in others. You might see a pastor or believer operate with striking accuracy in prophetic or revelatory gifts, yet be confused, misguided, or even blind in other aspects of their spiritual walk. Gifting in one area doesn't guarantee clarity in all areas—spiritual sensitivity must be cultivated holistically.

To Renew Your Mind Means:

- **To align your mind with God's mind**

Philippians 2:5
Let this mind be in you which was also in Christ Jesus,

1 Corinthians 2:16
"For 'who has known the mind of the Lord that he may instruct Him?' But we have the mind of Christ."

- **To think like God; to replace your thoughts with His; to adopt His point of view**

Isaiah 55:8
"For My thoughts are not your thoughts, Nor are your ways My ways," says the Lord.

Deuteronomy 11:18
"Therefore you shall lay up these words of mine in your heart and in your soul... and they shall be as frontlets between your eyes."

- **To be tuned to God's frequency, expecting to hear His voice**

Habakkuk 2:1
I will stand my watch And set myself on the rampart, And watch to see what He will say to me...

- **To control your thought life according to God's will**

Philippians 4:8
Finally, brethren, whatever things are true, noble, just, pure, lovely, of good report — if there is any virtue and anything praiseworthy — meditate on these things.

- **To arrest and destroy wrong thoughts**

2 Corinthians 10:5
casting down arguments and every high thing that

*exalts itself against the knowledge of God, bringing
every thought into captivity to the obedience of Christ.*

A **renewed mind is your responsibility**—and it is
essential to knowing God's will.

6. You Must Be Transformed or Spiritually Mature

Romans 12:2
*And do not be conformed to this world, but be transformed
by the renewing of your mind, that you may prove what is
that good and acceptable and perfect will of God.*

Transformation = Spiritual Maturity

The renewal of your mind must produce
transformation. Transformation is the **mark of
spiritual maturity,** and spiritual maturity is **essential
for discerning the voice of God.**

Natural Maturity Parallels Spiritual Maturity

In the natural, **babies don't recognize voices**
immediately. As they grow, they learn to recognize
their parents' voices and become selective about
whom they respond to.

Likewise, when you are first **born again**, you may not
recognize God's voice clearly. As you **mature
spiritually**, you will **discern His voice** in your spirit.

Hebrews 5:13-14
For everyone who partakes only of milk is unskilled in the word of righteousness, for he is a babe. 14 But solid food belongs to those who are of full age, that is, those who by reason of use have their senses exercised to discern both good and evil.

The "milk" and "meat" in this passage refer to the **written Word of God**. New believers begin with the **simple truths** (milk), but as they grow, they master **deeper truths** (meat).

The Result of Spiritual Maturity

- You will **develop your spiritual senses** to discern good and evil.
- You will **know the difference** between God's will and worldly ways.
- You will become **conformed to Christ**, not to worldly standards.
- You will gain **emotional maturity**, avoiding impulsive decisions made from anger or self-pity.

As you mature, you will also develop the **Fruit of the Spirit**, which is the evidence of both **spiritual and emotional maturity**.

7. You Must Understand God's Pattern of Communication With You

God Has a Unique Way of Communicating With Each Person

God establishes a **unique pattern of communication** with each of His children. While His Word is the same, the **way He deals with each person** often reflects their unique personality, background, and journey.

A Natural Example: Mothers and Their Children

Just as a mother may **love all her children equally but differently**, God also deals with **each of us individually**. From the outside, someone may think **one child is favored**, but the mother knows she is **responding to each child's uniqueness**.

God does the same with us. He **knows our uniqueness** and **communicates accordingly**.

You Must Learn How God Speaks to You Personally

- You must **learn and understand** how God uniquely communicates with you.
- You **cannot depend** on someone else to always hear God for you because they **may not understand how God deals with you personally**.

- Others may **confirm** God's voice, but you must be **directed primarily by what you hear yourself**.

Conclusion

To know God's voice, you must meet these **spiritual preconditions**:

1. Be born again
2. Be baptized in the Holy Spirit
3. Be spiritual
4. Be surrendered to His will
5. Continuously renew your mind
6. Be spiritually mature
7. Understand how God uniquely communicates with you

Chapter 4

How God Speaks

1 Kings 19:11-12
Then He said, "Go out, and stand on the mountain before the Lord." And behold, the Lord passed by, and a great and strong wind tore into the mountains and broke the rocks in pieces before the Lord, but the Lord was not in the wind; and after the wind an earthquake, but the Lord was not in the earthquake;
12 and after the earthquake a fire, but the Lord was not in the fire; and after the fire a still small voice."

Three Important Truths Before Exploring How God Speaks

1. We Must Learn How God Speaks to Recognize His Voice

Recognizing God's voice is essential for **understanding His will**. Success in life is knowing the will of God and walking in it.

Ephesians 5:17
Therefore do not be unwise, but understand what the will of the Lord is.

2. God Speaks in Many Ways

Our anchor text (1 Kings 19:11-12) demonstrates that God is not limited to one method of speaking.

- **Wind came — but God was not in the wind.**
  Elijah expected God in the wind, perhaps because God had spoken to him this way before.
- **An earthquake came — but God was not in the earthquake.**
  Again, Elijah expected God in the earthquake due to past experiences.
- **A fire came — but God was not in the fire.**
  Elijah had previously encountered God through fire, yet God was not in the fire this time.
- **Finally, a still small voice — and this time, God was in the voice.**
  God chose to speak in a **still small voice**.

This teaches us that **God is not confined to one method**. His way of speaking is determined by His **omniscience**.

Job 33:14
For God may speak in one way, or in another, Yet man does not perceive it.

3. Fellowship Is Key to Recognizing God's Voice

Fellowship is one of the most important keys to knowing God's voice.

2 Corinthians 13:14 (NIV)
May the grace of the Lord Jesus Christ, and the love of God, and the fellowship of the Holy Spirit be with you all.

Fellowship means **spending time with God** and with other believers.

Examples of fellowship:

- **Prayer and Bible study** – spending time with God
- **Church attendance** – fellowshipping with brethren
- **Meditation on the Word** – thinking about God
- **Worship through music** – praising God alone or with others
- **Evangelism** – sharing God's love with others

Fellowship **breeds familiarity**, familiarity **breeds understanding**, and understanding **enhances communication**. When two people understand each other, **few words are needed** for effective communication.

How God Speaks

God speaks **primarily through His Word**, both the **written Word (Logos)** and the **spoken Word (Rhema)**.

Hebrews 1:1-2
God, who at various times and in various ways spoke in

time past to the fathers by the prophets, 2 has in these last days spoken to us by His Son, whom He has appointed heir of all things, through whom also He made the worlds.

The **Word of God** is the primary vehicle of God's communication. Therefore, **every other form of revelation — dreams, visions, prophecy — must align with the Word.** If it contradicts the Word, it is **not from God**.

Mark 13:31
Heaven and earth will pass away, but My words will by no means pass away.

Everything must be tested by the Word of God, because only the Word **will never pass away**.

How God Speaks Through His Word

By Personal Revelation and Application

When you read the Bible and encounter a story or verse that **directly addresses your situation**, God is speaking to you. If you've been seeking an answer and find it in Scripture, that's God's voice.

The "Jumping Verse"

Sometimes, while reading Scripture, **a verse leaps off the page**, grabs your attention, and **stays on your mind**. This is often God **highlighting His message** to you.

The Ethiopian Eunuch's Encounter with the Word

Acts 8:31-35
And he said, "How can I, unless someone guides me?" And he asked Philip to come up and sit with him. The place in the Scripture which he read was this: "He was led as a sheep to the slaughter; And as a lamb before its shearer is silent, So He opened not His mouth. 33 In His humiliation His justice was taken away, And who will declare His generation? For His life is taken from the earth." 34 So the eunuch answered Philip and said, "I ask you, of whom does the prophet say this, of himself or of some other man?" 35 Then Philip opened his mouth, and beginning at this Scripture, preached Jesus to him.

The Word **spoke directly to his situation**, and **Philip explained** what God was saying.

The Written Word — God's Revealed Will

There are many things that God has already revealed in His **written Word** as His will for all believers. You do **not need special revelation** to act on them.

For example:

Mark 16:15-20
And He said to them, "Go into all the world and preach the gospel to every creature. 16 He who believes and is baptized will be saved; but he who does not believe will be condemned. 17 And these signs will follow those who believe: In My name they will cast out demons; they will

speak with new tongues; 18 they will take up serpents; and if they drink anything deadly, it will by no means hurt them; they will lay hands on the sick, and they will recover." 19 So then, after the Lord had spoken to them, He was received up into heaven, and sat down at the right hand of God. 20 And they went out and preached everywhere, the Lord working with them and confirming the word through the accompanying signs. Amen.

You **do not need special revelation** to share the Gospel or to pray for the sick — **it is already written**.

1 Thessalonians 5:18
In everything give thanks; for this is the will of God in Christ Jesus for you.

No matter your circumstances, **giving thanks** is **God's will**, and you don't need a vision or prophecy to obey this.

Spirit-Led or Anointed Preaching or Teaching

Jeremiah 3:15
And I will give you shepherds according to My heart, who will feed you with knowledge and understanding.

God speaks **through anointed preaching or teaching**. Right now, God is **speaking to you through my voice**. When you listen to sermons, teachings, or read books by anointed ministers, and the message **ministers to your situation**, it is often **God speaking to you**.

Anointed Counselors

Proverbs 11:14
Where there is no counsel, the people fall; But in the multitude of counselors there is safety.

When you seek counsel from **pastors, ministers, or fellow believers**, and they minister a word to you, it could be **God speaking through them**.

Many times, we **overlook familiar people** and **only listen to outsiders**, not realizing that **God speaks through those He has placed in our lives**. Your wife has been saying the same thing for months, but you did not think that was God until a pastor or a complete stranger says it, and suddenly you're excited acting like it's the first time you've heard it.

Example: Moses and Jethro

Even though God said He spoke to Moses **face to face**, He still used Moses' **father-in-law** to give him counsel.

Exodus 18:24-26
So Moses heeded the voice of his father-in-law and did all that he had said. 25 And Moses chose able men out of all Israel, and made them heads over the people: rulers of thousands, rulers of hundreds, rulers of fifties, and rulers of tens. 26 So they judged the people at all times; the hard cases they brought to Moses, but they judged every small case themselves.

God can speak through **anyone** — your spouse, children, friends, or even **unbelievers**. He once spoke to **Balaam through a donkey**.

Spirit-Led Interaction with Other Believers

Proverbs 27:17
As iron sharpens iron, So a man sharpens the countenance of his friend.

God can speak to you during **fellowship and conversation** with other believers. You might be in church, fellowship, or just talking with a friend when someone says **something that ministers directly to your situation**.

Example: Agabus and Paul; Acts 21:8-12

While Apostle Paul was staying with fellow believers at the home of Philip the Evangelist the prophet Agabus took Paul's belt, bound his own hands and feet with it, and declared, "This is how the owner of this belt will be bound and handed over to the authorities in Jerusalem." That was a prophetic word from God.

That's why, when the devil wants to destroy someone, he first isolates them — pulling them away from the fellowship of other believers through whom God might speak, correct, or intervene in their situation.

Anointed Music

God can speak through **anointed music**.

Job 35:10
10 But no one says, 'Where is God my Maker, Who gives songs in the night,'

Colossians 3:16
*Let the word of Christ dwell in you richly in all wisdom, teaching and admonishing one another **in psalms and hymns and spiritual songs, singing** with grace in your hearts to the Lord.*

Songs—both **Christian and sometimes even secular**—can carry **messages from God**. For instance, God once spoke to me through the hymn:
"O wait meekly wait and murmur not..."

Music **tunes your spirit to God's frequency** and allows His voice to be heard.

Meditation

Joshua 1:8
This Book of the Law shall not depart from your mouth, but you shall meditate in it day and night, that you may observe to do according to all that is written in it. For then you will make your way prosperous, and then you will have good success.

In Acts 10 Peter saw a vision and while he was meditating on what he saw the Holy Spirit spoke:

Acts 10:19-20
While Peter thought about the vision, the Spirit said to him, "Behold, three men are seeking you. 20 Arise therefore, go down and go with them, doubting nothing; for I have sent them."

Meditation is **chewing on the Word** until:

1. The **voice of God grows louder** within you than your doubts
2. **Light breaks forth** — you receive revelation
3. You just **know the truth** and **what to do**
4. The Word digests and becomes **part of your vocabulary, character, and constitution**
5. **Power is imparted** into your spirit
6. **Faith is born** regarding your situation

Faith comes not by reading or studying but by hearing (Romans 10:17:). Until the **Word becomes the Voice**, it cannot produce faith. And **faith is the victory** that overcomes the world.

1 John 5:4
For whatever is born of God overcomes the world. And this is the victory that has overcome the world — our faith.

Prayer

Father, in the name of Jesus, open the eyes of my understanding and that of every reader for insight into Your Word. Empower me and every member of this church to discern and recognize Your voice when You speak through those You have placed in our lives. Silence every noise in our lives that tries to drown out Your voice, and speak to us clearly in ways that we will understand, in the name of Jesus. *(Ephesians 1:17-19)*

Chapter 5

How God Speaks: Spiritual Signals

Job 33:14
For God may speak in one way, or in another, Yet man does not perceive it.

What Are Spiritual Signals?

A signal is a form of **communication** that is **wordless or coded,** understood through a pre-established agreement. For example, when you're driving and see a red light at an intersection, you stop—not because anyone told you to, but because there's a shared understanding of what that signal means. In the same way, spiritual signals are non-verbal cues or impressions God uses to communicate. In fact, God often speaks more through these subtle spiritual signals than through direct words. The issue is that many believers miss His voice simply because they don't recognize these signals as God speaking.

Acts 27:10
saying, "Men, I perceive that this voyage will end with disaster and much loss, not only of the cargo and ship, but also our lives."

How did Paul **perceive the danger** of the voyage? He felt something in his **spirit**. God **communicated** through a spiritual signal—perhaps a loss of peace, uneasiness, or inward check.

Spiritual signals are like God's body language. Just as you can read the body language of someone, you're close to, you can learn to discern what God is communicating without Him saying a word. For instance, your spouse might give you a certain look in public, and you immediately know it's time to leave. Or your child may carry themselves in a way that tells you something's wrong—even if they haven't said a word. We rely heavily on non-verbal cues with those we're close to, and it's the same with God. He's always communicating through spiritual signals, but only those who are intimately familiar with Him can recognize them. The deeper your relationship with God, the sharper your ability to pick up on His signals.

Acts 16:6-7
Now when they had gone through Phrygia and the region of Galatia, they were forbidden by the Holy Spirit to preach the word in Asia. 7 After they had come to Mysia, they tried to go into Bithynia, but the Spirit did not permit them.

How did the Spirit forbid them? The Bible does not say, likely because it was through spiritual signals. In the same chapter, Paul later received a vision (v.9), but in verses 6–7, it was likely internal sensing.

Acts 16:9

9 And a vision appeared to Paul in the night. A man of Macedonia stood and pleaded with him, saying, "Come over to Macedonia and help us."

Spiritual signals are not the same as emotions. Many people confuse the two because spiritual signals often involve a perception or inner impression that feels similar to emotion. For example, the Apostle Paul perceived in his spirit that the voyage ahead would be dangerous. That wasn't a fear-based emotion—it was a spiritual alert. Or consider when your wife senses that a business transaction doesn't feel right, or you suddenly feel burdened about your son who's thousands of miles away in Canada. These are typical ways spiritual signals manifest: subtle, internal impressions that seem like feelings but are much deeper.

The confusion arises because these signals are often accompanied by emotion—but they are not caused by emotion. Emotions are generated by the flesh. They're triggered by external stimuli: something you saw, heard, experienced, or remembered. Emotions respond to carnal inputs and are rooted in the soul.

Spiritual signals, on the other hand, are internally generated—from the spirit man. They may be responses to events, but they originate from deep within, often as a stirring or friction in your spirit in communion with the Spirit of God. While emotions react to the outside world, spiritual signals flow from your spirit, often without any obvious external trigger. And although they may produce emotional responses, their root is spiritual, not soulish.

- Emotions: *Carnal, external stimulus*
- Spiritual signals: *Spiritual, internal awareness*

Spiritual signals are evidence of intimacy with God. The **more intimate you are with God,** the more you can **recognize and respond to His signals** — just like **a spouse or child's body language** becomes clear through closeness.

Types of Spiritual Signals

1. Conscience

God speaks through your **conscience**.

Romans 9:1
I tell the truth in Christ, I am not lying, my conscience also bearing me witness in the Holy Spirit.

Conscience is the inner guide that either approves or disapproves your actions. It functions as an internal signal, measuring your behavior against a value system and alerting you when something aligns — or conflicts — with it.

Romans 2:15
who show the work of the law written in their hearts, their conscience also bearing witness, and between themselves their thoughts accusing or else excusing them)

Conscience is an internal standard by which our thoughts and actions are measured—either approved or condemned. It's one of the ways God speaks to us and guides our decisions.

The Bible Warns That Conscience Can Be Compromised

Weak Conscience – repeated violations weaken conscience.

1 Corinthians 8:12
But when you thus sin against the brethren, and wound their weak conscience, you sin against Christ.

Defiled Conscience – corrupted by sin

Titus 1:15
To the pure all things are pure, but to those who are defiled and unbelieving nothing is pure; but even their mind and conscience are defiled.

Seared Conscience – hardened beyond sensitivity

1 Timothy 4:2
speaking lies in hypocrisy, having their own conscience seared with a hot iron,

Clear Conscience - When your conscience is polluted or compromised, it may no longer reflect the will of God accurately. A clear conscience doesn't always mean you're innocent—it simply means your inner gauge may be misaligned.

1 Corinthians 4:4 (NIV)
My conscience is clear, but that does not make me innocent. It is the Lord who judges me.

Conditions for Conscience to Be a Reliable Signal from God

- **It must be pure**
  1 Timothy 3:9
  holding the mystery of the faith with a pure conscience.
- **It must be good**
  1 Timothy 1:5
  Now the purpose of the commandment is love from a pure heart, from a good conscience, and from sincere faith.
- **It must be free of offense**
  Acts 24:16
  This being so, I myself always strive to have a conscience without offense toward God and men.
- **It must be cleansed from dead works**
  Hebrews 9:14
  how much more shall the blood of Christ, who through the eternal Spirit offered Himself without spot to God, cleanse your conscience from dead works to serve the living God?

- **It must be powered by the Word and the Holy Spirit**
  Romans 9:1
  I tell the truth in Christ, I am not lying, my conscience also bearing me witness in the Holy Spirit.

2. Burdens

God often speaks through **burdens** — a strong spiritual **urge, concern, or weight** that guides you into **divine action**.

Malachi 1:1
The burden of the word of the Lord to Israel by Malachi.

A burden is a **spiritual weight, a deep passion,** or an **intense concern** that God impresses upon your heart to **draw your attention to something** He desires to accomplish. It's as if God transfers His own **feelings about a matter into you** — so you begin to feel what He feels. That shared sense of urgency or concern stirs you to act in alignment with His purpose.

Jesus Described It as a Yoke and Burden

Matthew 11:29-30
Take My yoke upon you and learn from Me, for I am gentle and lowly in heart, and you will find rest for your souls. 30 For My yoke is easy and My burden is light."

God's burdens are not oppressive — they are **motivating, divine concerns** that align us with His will.

Examples of Burden as a Spiritual Signal

- Have you ever felt the **urge to pray** for someone out of nowhere?
- Have you ever had a **strong prompting to help someone**, to go somewhere, or to make a call? These are likely **burdens from God**.

Testimony Example

A man was **trapped in a ditch late at night**. A nearby believer couldn't sleep — he was **stirred to pray**, then had a **sudden urge to drive out**, found the trapped man, and called 911 to rescue him. That was **God speaking through a burden**.

Example: Phinehas Zealous with God's Zeal

Numbers 25:11
"Phinehas the son of Eleazar, the son of Aaron the priest, has turned back My wrath from the children of Israel, because he was zealous with My zeal among them, so that I did not consume the children of Israel in My zeal."

Phinehas **felt God's indignation** and acted decisively. That's a **burden in action**.

Compassion as a Burden

Jesus often healed people because He was **moved with compassion** — the **burden of love** from God for people.

Mark 1:41
Then Jesus, moved with compassion, stretched out His hand and touched him, and said to him, "I am willing; be cleansed."

Compassion is a powerful spiritual signal that activates divine intervention.

Common Types of Burdens

- **Burden to pray** for someone or something
- **Burden for souls** — evangelism, outreach
- **Burden to help** — serving or giving
- **Righteous indignation** — anger at injustice or sin
- Many discover their **callings and ministries** through burdens
- Burdens can also lead to **prophetic utterances** (e.g., Malachi, Isaiah)

3. Spiritual Impressions

God speaks through **spiritual impressions**, often described as a **"knowing" signal**.

Acts 27:10
saying, "Men, I perceive that this voyage will end with disaster and much loss, not only of the cargo and ship, but also our lives."

Paul **perceived** danger—not through logic, but through **a direct spiritual impression**.

What Is a Spiritual Impression?

A spiritual impression is often referred to as a "knowing signal." It's that unexplainable inner awareness—you just know, even though you can't trace how you came to that knowledge. It's a sudden insight or understanding that enters your spirit through a supernatural channel, updating your perception without any natural explanation.

It is a **direct sense of truth or fact**—a **knowing** that does not come from **reasoning or analysis** but from **your spirit**. It is the ability to know something without relying on **logical reasoning** or **analytical thought**. It's an **inner awareness** that bypasses the natural mind and flows directly from **the spirit**.

Luke 6:8
But He knew their thoughts, and said to the man who had the withered hand, "Arise and stand here." And he arose and stood.

Mark 2:8
But immediately, when Jesus perceived in His spirit that they reasoned thus within themselves, He said to them, "Why do you reason about these things in your hearts?"

Luke 5:22
But when Jesus perceived their thoughts, He answered and said to them, "Why are you reasoning in your hearts?"

Luke 8:46
But Jesus said, "Somebody touched Me, for I perceived power going out from Me."

These scriptures show Jesus **knew things directly through His spirit**, without conversation or visible signs.

Spiritual Impressions in Daily Life

- You **walk into a room** and suddenly feel **uneasy** or **alert**.
- Your **daughter is far away**, but you suddenly sense something is wrong.
- You **just know** something is true without any natural way of knowing.

In all these cases, God is **speaking through spiritual impressions**.

4. Inward Witness

One of the most **common spiritual signals** is the **inward witness**, often experienced as **peace** or the **absence of peace**.

Psalm 85:8
I will hear what God the Lord will speak, For He will speak

peace To His people and to His saints; But let them not turn back to folly.

God Uses Peace to Guide and Guard You

Colossians 3:15
And let the peace of God rule in your hearts, to which also you were called in one body; and be thankful.

The word **"rule"** here means **to act as an umpire** — peace serves as a **signal** of God's direction.

Philippians 4:7
and the peace of God, which surpasses all understanding, will guard your hearts and minds through Christ Jesus.

Peace acts as a **guardian** of your heart and mind. When peace is present, it often means **God is affirming your path**. When peace is absent, it could be **God's warning signal**.

Examples of Inward Witness

- When you're about to make a decision (job, marriage, travel) and your **heart is troubled**, God may be **speaking through lack of peace**.
- Conversely, when circumstances are chaotic but you feel **unexplainable peace**, that may be **God affirming your path**.

While **peace** is the **most common inward witness,** God also speaks through **joy, conviction, and assurance**, but peace is the **primary signal**.

Summary of How Spiritual Signals Work Together

Each spiritual signal performs a **specific function** in communicating God's will:

Conscience – Helps discern **right from wrong**

Burdens – Reveal what you should **care about or act upon**

Spiritual Impressions – Provide **instant knowing** or understanding beyond logic

Inward Witness – Offers **peace or unrest** to guide decisions and responses

God speaks to provoke a response from you. His communication is not just for information—it's meant to produce action. Your ability to recognize, interpret, and respond to spiritual signals depends on the strength and maturity of your spirit. That's why Paul prayed in Ephesians 3:16 that we would be *"strengthened with might by His Spirit in the inner man."* A strong spirit is essential for discerning and responding accurately to the voice of God.

Attitudes (Spirits) That Promote Sensitivity to Spiritual Signals

1. **A Contrite Spirit** – This refers to a spirit of brokenness before God—a heart that is humbled, repentant, and deeply aware of its need for Him. It is crushed in pride but rich in dependence, longing fully for God's presence and guidance.

   Psalm 34:18
   The Lord is near to those who have a broken heart,
   And saves such as have a contrite spirit.

2. **A Meek and Quiet Spirit** – A humble, gentle spirit that reverently trembles at God's Word. It is selfless in nature, consistently placing others above itself and walking in quiet submission to God's authority.

   1 Peter 3:4 (KJV)
   But let it be the hidden man of the heart, in that which is not corruptible, even the ornament of a meek and quiet spirit, which is in the sight of God of great price.

3. **A Fervent Spirit** – A strong, vibrant, enthusiastic, and joyful spirit—full of life and energy—stands in stark contrast to a spirit that is indifferent, depressed, weak, and emotionally suppressed.

Romans 12:11 (KJV)
Not slothful in business; fervent in spirit; serving the Lord;

Attitudes (Spirits) That Hinder Sensitivity to Spiritual Signals

1. **An Unfaithful Spirit** – This describes an immature, unstable, and unreliable spirit — easily swayed by every wind of doctrine and carried off by empty philosophies.

   Psalm 78:8
   And may not be like their fathers, A stubborn and rebellious generation, A generation that did not set its heart aright, And whose spirit was not faithful to God.

2. **A Hasty Spirit** – This is a restless, impatient spirit — like that of King Saul — who failed to wait on God's timing.

   Proverbs 14:29 (KJV)
   29 He that is slow to wrath is of great understanding: but he that is hasty of spirit exalteth folly.

3. **A Haughty Spirit** – This is a proud, arrogant spirit — puffed up with self-importance — often dismissing spiritual signals and masking ignorance as knowledge through rationalization.

Proverbs 16:18
Pride goes before destruction, And a haughty spirit before a fall.

Prayers

Prayer 1
Father, in the name of Jesus, cleanse my conscience and that of every reader, so that our consciences will be accurate indicators of Your will. Empower each of us with grace to recognize and respond to Your burdens. Sharpen our sensitivity to spiritual impressions and signals, in the name of Jesus. *(Hebrews 9:14; Matthew 11:29-30)*

Prayer 2
Father, in the name of Jesus, let everything in my life and in the life of every reader that hinders our capacity to understand and respond to spiritual signals be terminated today. Strengthen our inner man by Your Spirit. Create in us contrite hearts and steadfast spirits. Multiply the fervency and vibrancy of our spirits. Clothe us with meek and quiet spirits, in the name of Jesus. *(Ephesians 3:16; Psalm 51:10; Psalm 34:18; Psalm 78:8; Proverbs 14:29; Proverbs 16:18; Romans 12:11; 1 Peter 3:4)*

Chapter 6

How God Speaks: Voices

1 Kings 19:11-12
Then He said, "Go out, and stand on the mountain before the Lord." And behold, the Lord passed by, and a great and strong wind tore into the mountains and broke the rocks in pieces before the Lord, but the Lord was not in the wind; and after the wind an earthquake, but the Lord was not in the earthquake;
12 and after the earthquake a fire, but the Lord was not in the fire; and after the fire a still small voice.

At the beginning of this book, we established that **God speaks in many ways**. He is not limited to a single mode of communication.

Job 33:14
For God may speak in one way, or in another, Yet man does not perceive it.

One of the **most profound ways** God speaks is through **voices**. Many people throughout history have **heard His voice** and continue to do so. Jesus made this clear:

John 10:27
My sheep hear My voice, and I know them, and they follow Me.

Two Types of Voices with Which God Speaks

1. The Audible Voice of God

This refers to **hearing God's voice with your physical ears** —just as you hear a friend or spouse speak. It sounds **external and real,** as though someone is physically present with you.

Biblical Examples of the Audible Voice of God

- **God spoke to Moses audibly at the burning bush**:
  Exodus 3:4
  4 So when the Lord saw that he turned aside to look, God called to him from the midst of the bush and said, "Moses, Moses!" And he said, "Here I am."
- **God spoke to Saul (later Paul) on the Damascus road audibly**:
  Acts 9:3-5
  As he journeyed he came near Damascus, and suddenly a light shone around him from heaven. 4Then he fell to the ground, and heard a voice saying to him, "Saul, Saul, why are you persecuting Me?" 5 And he said, "Who are You, Lord?" Then the Lord said, "I am Jesus, whom you are persecuting. It is hard for you to kick against the goads."

- **God called Samuel audibly**:
  1 Samuel 3:10
  Now the Lord came and stood and called as at other times, "Samuel! Samuel!" And Samuel answered, "Speak, for Your servant hears."
- **God spoke about Jesus at His baptism and transfiguration audibly.**
  Matthew 3:16-17
  When He had been baptized, Jesus came up immediately from the water; and behold, the heavens were opened to Him, and He saw the Spirit of God descending like a dove and alighting upon Him. 17 And suddenly a voice came from heaven, saying, "This is My beloved Son, in whom I am well pleased."

Matthew 17:5-6
While he was still speaking, behold, a bright cloud overshadowed them; and suddenly a voice came out of the cloud, saying, "This is My beloved Son, in whom I am well pleased. Hear Him!" 6 And when the disciples heard it, they fell on their faces and were greatly afraid.

Important Notes on the Audible Voice

- Every time the Bible says *"And God said"* or *"God commanded"*, it often refers to an **audible voice**.
- When God speaks audibly, **people around you may or may not hear it**:
  - With Paul:
    Acts 9:7

> *And the men who journeyed with him stood
> speechless, hearing a voice but seeing no one.*
> - With Jesus' transfiguration:
>   **Matthew 17:6**
>   *And when the disciples heard it, they fell on
>   their faces and were greatly afraid.*
- Sometimes **God's audible voice may sound like
  someone familiar** — a pastor, mentor, or parent.
  - With Samuel, **God's voice sounded like
    Eli's**:
    1 Samuel 3:3-8
    *(Verses detail how Samuel ran to Eli multiple
    times, thinking Eli had called him.)*
- God **still speaks audibly today**, but **less
  frequently** than through the **inner voice** of the
  Holy Spirit.

2. The Inner Voice of the Holy Spirit

This is the **most common way God speaks** to His
people. It is a **spiritual voice**, heard within your **heart
or spirit** — not with your physical ears but with
spiritual ears.

In many places where the Bible says, "And the Spirit
said," or "The word of the Lord came to me," it is most
likely referring to the inner voice of the Holy Spirit
speaking within a person's spirit.

Biblical Examples of the Inner Voice

- **Acts 10:19-20**
  While Peter thought about the vision, the Spirit said to him, "Behold, three men are seeking you. 20 Arise therefore, go down and go with them, doubting nothing; for I have sent them."
- **Acts 8:29**
  Then the Spirit said to Philip, "Go near and overtake this chariot."
- **Ezekiel 11:5**
  Then the Spirit of the Lord fell upon me, and said to me, "Speak! 'Thus says the Lord: "Thus you have said, O house of Israel; for I know the things that come into your mind."'

Characteristics of the Inner Voice

- It is the **voice within you** — usually **gentle**, sometimes **firm** (especially with warnings or commands).
- It may come as a **thought** or a **conversation** within.
- This is the voice you hear in your heart as you study and meditate on Scripture — rising gently through the Word, in fulfillment of Psalm 29:3.

Psalm 29:3
The voice of the Lord is over the waters;
("Waters" here symbolically refer to the **Word of God**.)

The Inner Voice Is Key to Spiritual Guidance

John 16:13
However, when He, the Spirit of truth, has come, He will guide you into all truth; for He will not speak on His own authority, but whatever He hears He will speak; and He will tell you things to come.

This inner voice **teaches, guides**, and **warns** — as Jesus promised.

Romans 8:14
For as many as are led by the Spirit of God, these are sons of God.

Hearing and following the inner voice is what it means to be **led by the Spirit**.

Activation Tip

You must **train your soul** to hear this voice through:

- **Meditating on God's Word**
- **Praying in the Spirit abundantly**

Prayer

Father, in the name of Jesus, let everything **blocking my natural ears, spiritual ears, and my heart** from hearing and recognizing Your voice be **roasted by fire today**. Let everything **hindering every reader** from hearing Your voice be destroyed. **Open our ears and hearts** to the voice of Your Spirit from henceforth, in

Jesus' name. *(Proverbs 2:2; 4:20; Isaiah 6:10; Revelation 2:11a)*

Chapter 7

How God Speaks: Dreams and Visions

Numbers 12:6
Then He said, "Hear now My words: If there is a prophet among you, I, the Lord, make Myself known to him in a vision; I speak to him in a dream."

Important Things You Should Know About Dreams and Visions

1. There Are Various Kinds of Dreams and Visions

Scripture reveals that **dreams and visions vary** in nature, purpose, and form.

Daniel 1:17
As for these four young men, God gave them knowledge and skill in all literature and wisdom; and Daniel had understanding in all visions and dreams.

2. Dreams and Visions Are Among the Most Common Ways God Speaks to Everyone — Including Unbelievers

Job 33:14–17

For God may speak in one way, or in another, Yet man does not perceive it. 15 In a dream, in a vision of the night, When deep sleep falls upon men, While slumbering on their beds, 16 Then He opens the ears of men, And seals their instruction. 17 In order to turn man from his deed, And conceal pride from man,

Examples:

- **God spoke to Abimelech, a pagan king, in a dream**:
  Genesis 20:3
  But God came to Abimelech in a dream by night, and said to him, "Indeed you are a dead man because of the woman whom you have taken, for she is a man's wife."
- **God revealed world events to Nebuchadnezzar in a dream**:
  Daniel 2:1
  Now in the second year of Nebuchadnezzar's reign, Nebuchadnezzar had dreams; and his spirit was so troubled that his sleep left him.
- **God spoke to Pharaoh through dreams about a coming famine**:
  Genesis 41:1
  Then it came to pass, at the end of two full years, that Pharaoh had a dream; and behold, he stood by the river.
- **Cornelius received an open vision**:
  Acts 10:3
  About the ninth hour of the day he saw clearly in a

vision an angel of God coming in and saying to him, "Cornelius!"

3. Everyone Is Wired to Dream and See Visions

- Dreams and visions are **spiritual faculties** given to every person. If you are **not dreaming** or **do not remember your dreams**, it could indicate spiritual interference or bondage.
- Lack of dreams or memory of dreams may result from **inattention** or **demonic attack** on your dream life.
- Today, by faith in Christ, you are **released from every bondage affecting your dream life**, and your capacity to dream, see visions, and remember them is **restored in Jesus' name**.

4. Transactions in Dreams and Visions Are Real and Impact Reality

- **Solomon received wisdom, wealth, and honor through a dream**:
  1 Kings 3:11–15
  11 Then God said to him: "Because you have asked this thing, and have not asked long life for yourself, nor have asked riches for yourself, nor have asked the life of your enemies, but have asked for yourself understanding to discern justice, 12 behold, I have done according to your words; see, I have given you a wise and understanding heart, so that there has not been anyone like you before you, nor shall any like

you arise after you. 13 And I have also given you what you have not asked: both riches and honor, so that there shall not be anyone like you among the kings all your days. 14 So if you walk in My ways, to keep My statutes and My commandments, as your father David walked, then I will lengthen your days." 15 Then Solomon awoke; and indeed it had been a dream. And he came to Jerusalem and stood before the ark of the covenant of the Lord, offered up burnt offerings, offered peace offerings, and made a feast for all his servants.

- **The butler and the baker in Joseph's prison had dreams that foretold their fate**:
  (Genesis 40:6–23 — refer for detailed narrative)
- **King Belshazzar saw the fall of his kingdom in a vision**:
  (Daniel 5:1–31 — within 24 hours, the vision manifested.)
- Many have experienced powerful encounters in dreams — both negative and positive. Some have eaten in a dream and woken up physically ill; others have been attacked and awakened with visible marks from the assault. Yet, there are also those who were prayed for in a dream and woke up healed, or were rescued in a dream and woke up delivered. These experiences reveal the reality and impact of spiritual encounters in the dream realm.

5. Dreams and Visions Are Not Final, they Can Be Changed by the Word of God

However, dreams and visions are not absolute. They can be altered, canceled, or overturned by faith in the Word of God. In every case, God's Word holds the final authority—it is greater than any dream or vision and has the power to nullify or render them ineffective.

Jeremiah 23:28
"The prophet who has a dream, let him tell a dream; And he who has My word, let him speak My word faithfully. What is the chaff to the wheat?" says the Lord.

The **dream is the chaff**, the **Word of God is the wheat**. Dreams can be **cancelled or altered** if they contradict God's word. So if you dream of dying prematurely, recognize that it contradicts the Word of God. Scripture declares, "You shall serve the Lord your God... and He will fulfill the number of your days" (Exodus 23:25–26). Therefore, cancel that dream by standing on God's Word and reject it with authority. It has no power over you when you walk in covenant truth.

6. Dreams and Visions Are Not God's Preferred Method of Speaking

- God **prefers to speak directly** through His Word, audible voice, or spiritual signals.

- Dreams and visions are **secondary**, often used when direct communication is ignored.
- There is no record of God speaking to Jesus through dreams or visions. When visions occurred during His ministry, they were for the benefit of others, not for His own guidance.
- God's communication with Adam was direct and personal—not through dreams or visions. Scripture says He spoke with Adam as they walked together in the cool of the day.
- Most of God's interactions with Abraham were also clear and direct, not primarily through dreams or visions.
- Similarly, God spoke to Moses face to face, with clarity—not through dreams or symbolic visions.

Numbers 12:6–8
Then He said, "Hear now My words: If there is a prophet among you, I, the Lord, make Myself known to him in a vision; I speak to him in a dream. 7 Not so with My servant Moses; He is faithful in all My house. 8 I speak with him face to face, Even plainly, and not in dark sayings; And he sees the form of the Lord. Why then were you not afraid To speak against My servant Moses?"

God is making it clear that while He often speaks to people through dreams and visions, He reserves direct and clear communication for those who walk in close intimacy with Him. In other words, the deeper your relationship with God, the less He relies on dreams and visions to speak to you. The more intimate and valuable you are to Him, the more clearly and directly He communicates with you.

This principle is seen in the life of Jesus. When He walked the earth, He spoke to the crowds in parables, but to His disciples—those closest to Him—He spoke plainly and without veils.

It's important to understand that dreams and visions are not God's highest or preferred method of communication. Many mistakenly believe that unless something comes through a dream, or vision, it isn't truly from God—even when it's clearly written in Scripture. They treat supernatural experiences as more valid than the Word itself.

However, Job 33:14-24 outlines a progression in how God speaks to man—showing that direct communication is available, but when that is missed or ignored, God may resort to dreams and visions as secondary measures to get our attention.

Job 33:14-24
14 For God may speak in one way, or in another, Yet man does not perceive it. 15 In a dream, in a vision of the night, When deep sleep falls upon men, While slumbering on their beds, 16 Then He opens the ears of men, And seals their instruction. 17 In order to turn man from his deed, And conceal pride from man, 18 He keeps back his soul from the Pit, And his life from [a]perishing by the sword. 19 "Man is also chastened with pain on his bed, And with strong pain

in many of his bones, 20 So that his life abhors bread, And his soul [b]succulent food. 21 His flesh wastes away from sight, And his bones stick out which once were not seen. 22 Yes, his soul draws near the Pit, And his life to the executioners. 23 "If there is a messenger for him, A mediator, one among a thousand, To show man His uprightness, 24 Then He is gracious to him, and says, 'Deliver him from going down to the Pit; I have found [c]a ransom';

Job 33:14–24 (summarized structure):

1. God speaks **clearly first** (v14)
2. Then through **dreams/visions** (v15-18)
3. Then through **circumstances** (v19-22)
4. Finally through **a messenger/prophet** (v23-24)

For example, God may have spoken to you clearly — whether through the inner voice, audible voice, or spiritual signals — telling you to leave a particular job. But you ignored Him. Then He confirmed it through a dream or vision, yet you still didn't pay attention. Eventually, your boss fired you, and even then, you failed to see God's hand in the situation. Finally, God sends a prophet or messenger to speak a word of knowledge or prophecy, helping you understand what He's been trying to communicate all along.

This is why prophecy often comes as confirmation. In many cases, when you hear a prophetic word, it feels familiar — because God has already spoken it to your spirit before.

In fact, as a principle, God usually won't send someone else to speak to you about a matter unless He has first tried to speak to you directly. When you're not responsive to His direct communication, He may send another voice to confirm or clarify what He's already said — so you'll believe and act.

7. Dreams and Visions Require Spiritual Interpretation and Only The Holy Spirit Can Interpret them.

Genesis 40:8
And they said to him, "We each have had a dream, and there is no interpreter of it." So Joseph said to them, "Do not interpretations belong to God? Tell them to me, please."

Daniel 9:21–23
yes, while I was speaking in prayer, the man Gabriel, whom I had seen in the vision at the beginning, being caused to fly swiftly, reached me about the time of the evening offering.
22 And he informed me, and talked with me, and said, "O Daniel, I have now come forth to give you skill to understand.
23 At the beginning of your supplications the command went out, and I have come to tell you, for you are greatly beloved; therefore consider the matter, and understand the vision:"

Joel 2:28

"And it shall come to pass afterward That I will pour out My Spirit on all flesh; Your sons and your daughters shall prophesy, Your old men shall dream dreams, Your young men shall see visions.

Prayer

Father, in the name of Jesus, by the operation of the Holy Spirit, give me and every reader **seeing eyes**, **hearing ears**, and **understanding hearts** that we may comprehend and discern your communication through dreams and visions in the name of Jesus **Joel 2:28**

Chapter 8

How God Speaks: Types of Visions

1 Samuel 3:1 (KJV)
And the child Samuel ministered unto the Lord before Eli. And the word of the Lord was precious in those days; there was no open vision.

Introduction

In the previous chapter, we explored how God speaks through **dreams and visions**. In this chapter, we will go deeper by examining the **various kinds of visions** through which God communicates. There are **four primary types** of visions in Scripture.

1. Inner Vision or Spiritual Vision

An inner vision, also called a spiritual vision, is a picture or scene you perceive with the eyes of your heart—your spiritual eyes—without your natural senses being suspended. The vision takes place within you, not outside of you, and you "see" it inwardly through your spirit.

This is the most common type of vision and often happens during spiritually engaging activities such as prayer, fasting, speaking in tongues, worship, or meditation. In those moments, an image may form in your spirit, or a scene may flash across your inner consciousness like a movie—brief, vivid, and spiritually significant.

Example: Elisha and Gehazi.

When Gehazi went behind Prophet Elisha to collect gifts from Naaman, Prophet Elisha saw it in a spiritual vision.

2 Kings 5:25–26
Now he went in and stood before his master. Elisha said to him, "Where did you go, Gehazi?" And he said, "Your servant did not go anywhere." 26 Then he said to him, "Did not my heart go with you when the man turned back from his chariot to meet you? Is it time to receive money and to receive clothing, olive groves and vineyards, sheep and oxen, male and female servants?"

An inner vision occurs when a picture, image, or scene floats into your inner consciousness while your physical senses remain fully alert. You are not dreaming or in a trance, yet you "see" something within. These visions occur in the mind's eye, or the eyes of your heart, and are typically sourced from your spirit.

These visions can come from either God or the devil. A vision from God is often a spontaneous image released from your regenerated spirit into your conscious awareness. For example, I once walked into someone's home and suddenly saw an image of him selling cars — even though that wasn't his profession at the time. I asked, "Why aren't you selling cars?" He replied that the thought had crossed his mind, but he hadn't taken it seriously. Not long after, he launched a successful car business. That's the power of a God-sent inner vision.

Symbolic or Figurative Visions

Sometimes inner visions are symbolic. For instance, during deliverance sessions, I often see animals that represent specific spirits or strongholds. These images are not random; they carry spiritual meaning.

Unfortunately, many people dismiss such images — especially when they are symbolic — because they lack the understanding to interpret them. But dismissing a vision due to lack of understanding can cause you to miss divine direction.

Sources of Inner Visions Created by Imagination

Not all inner visions come from God directly. Some are formed by your imagination — and their power and accuracy depend on their source. Here's how to evaluate them:

From Someone Speaking to You

If a vision forms while someone is talking, the source of that vision is likely the speaker — unless they are speaking by the Spirit of God.

From Your Own Desires

If the image is shaped by your personal longings or ambitions, then you are the source of the vision.

From the Word of God

If the vision arises while you're meditating on Scripture, then God is the source.

Psalm 119:18 says, "Open my eyes, that I may see wondrous things from Your law."

From Negative Influences

If it comes from consuming toxic or fearful content (like horror movies), then the vision likely originates from the devil.

The Power and Impact of Inner Visions

- The source of a vision determines its power and authenticity.
- The effectiveness of a vision also depends on your faith in it.

For example, if you form a mental picture while meditating on Scripture and believe it, no devil can stop it from coming to pass. In Genesis 11:6, God

Himself said of the builders of Babel,
"Nothing they imagine to do will be withheld from them."

This shows that your imagination is a spiritual tool — a barometer of God's performance in your life. When guided by the Spirit and rooted in the Word, it becomes a channel for divine manifestation.

Ephesians 3:20 (NIV)
Now to him who is able to do immeasurably more than all we ask or imagine, according to his power that is at work within us.

2. Open Vision

In an open vision, what is being revealed appears before you as if projected on a screen, right in front of your eyes. Your physical senses remain fully alert — you are awake and aware of your surroundings — but at the same time, you are seeing into the realm of the spirit. It's a supernatural overlay on the natural, where the spiritual breaks into the visible without suspending your natural awareness.

Example: Cornelius' Open Vision

Acts 10:3-4
About the ninth hour of the day he saw clearly in a vision an

angel of God coming in and saying to him, "Cornelius!" 4 And when he observed him, he was afraid, and said, "What is it, lord?" So he said to him, "Your prayers and your alms have come up for a memorial before God."

Example: The Mount of Transfiguration

Matthew 17:1–9

Now after six days Jesus took Peter, James, and John his brother, led them up on a high mountain by themselves; 2 and He was transfigured before them. His face shone like the sun, and His clothes became as white as the light. 3 And behold, Moses and Elijah appeared to them, talking with Him. 4 Then Peter answered and said to Jesus, "Lord, it is good for us to be here; if You wish, let us make here three tabernacles: one for You, one for Moses, and one for Elijah." 5 While he was still speaking, behold, a bright cloud overshadowed them; and suddenly a voice came out of the cloud, saying, "This is My beloved Son, in whom I am well pleased. Hear Him!" 6 And when the disciples heard it, they fell on their faces and were greatly afraid. 7 But Jesus came and touched them and said, "Arise, and do not be afraid." 8 When they had lifted up their eyes, they saw no one but Jesus only. 9 Now as they came down from the mountain, Jesus commanded them, saying, "Tell the vision to no one until the Son of Man is risen from the dead."

Example: Paul on the Road to Damascus

Acts 9:3–7

As he journeyed he came near Damascus, and suddenly a light shone around him from heaven. 4 Then he fell to the ground, and heard a voice saying to him, "Saul, Saul, why are you persecuting Me?" 5 And he said, "Who are You, Lord?" Then the Lord said, "I am Jesus, whom you are persecuting. It is hard for you to kick against the goads." 6 So he, trembling and astonished, said, "Lord, what do You want me to do?" Then the Lord said to him, "Arise and go into the city, and you will be told what you must do." 7 And the men who journeyed with him stood speechless, hearing a voice but seeing no one.

3. Visitation

Visitations are divine encounters where **God or His angels interact with you directly**. While not strictly visions, they are often classified as such due to their **supernatural nature**.

Example: Moses' Face-to-Face Encounter

Numbers 12:6–8
Then He said, "Hear now My words: If there is a prophet among you, I, the Lord, make Myself known to him in a vision; I speak to him in a dream. 7 Not so with My servant Moses; He is faithful in all My house. 8 I speak with him face to face, Even plainly, and not in dark sayings; And he sees the form of the Lord. Why then were you not afraid To speak against My servant Moses?"

Example: God Visiting Abraham

Genesis 18:1–5

Then the Lord appeared to him by the terebinth trees of Mamre, as he was sitting in the tent door in the heat of the day. 2 So he lifted his eyes and looked, and behold, three men were standing by him; and when he saw them, he ran from the tent door to meet them, and bowed himself to the ground, 3 and said, "My Lord, if I have now found favor in Your sight, do not pass on by Your servant. 4 Please let a little water be brought, and wash your feet, and rest yourselves under the tree. 5 And I will bring a morsel of bread, that you may refresh your hearts. After that you may pass by, inasmuch as you have come to your servant." They said, "Do as you have said."

Example: Peter's Angelic Visitation

Acts 12:5–10

Peter was therefore kept in prison, but constant prayer was offered to God for him by the church. 6 And when Herod was about to bring him out, that night Peter was sleeping, bound with two chains between two soldiers; and the guards before the door were keeping the prison. 7 Now behold, an angel of the Lord stood by him, and a light shone in the prison; and he struck Peter on the side and raised him up, saying, "Arise quickly!" And his chains fell off his hands. 8 Then the angel said to him, "Gird yourself and tie on your sandals"; and so he did. And he said to him, "Put on your garment and follow me." 9 So he went out and followed him, and did not know that what was done by the angel was real, but thought he was seeing a vision. 10 When they were past the first and the second guard posts, they came to the iron gate that leads to the city, which opened to them of its own accord; and they went out and went down one street, and immediately the angel departed from him.

4. Trance

In a trance, your natural senses are suspended, and you are fully immersed in the realm of the vision. You lose awareness of your physical surroundings and become entirely conscious of the spiritual dimension. If you see an angel in a trance, you perceive that angel in the context of the spirit realm — not in relation to the physical world around you.

Example: Paul's Heavenly Vision

2 Corinthians 12:1–4
It is doubtless not profitable for me to boast. I will come to visions and revelations of the Lord: 2 I know a man in Christ who fourteen years ago — whether in the body I do not know, or whether out of the body I do not know, God knows — such a one was caught up to the third heaven. 3 And I know such a man — whether in the body or out of the body I do not know, God knows — 4 how he was caught up into Paradise and heard inexpressible words, which it is not lawful for a man to utter.

Example: Peter's Vision of Clean and Unclean Animals

Acts 10:10–16
Then he became very hungry and wanted to eat; but while they made ready, he fell into a trance 11 and saw heaven opened and an object like a great sheet bound at the four corners, descending to him and let down to the earth. 12 In it were all kinds of four-footed animals of the earth, wild beasts, creeping things, and birds of the air. 13 And a voice came to him, "Rise, Peter; kill and eat." 14 But Peter said, "Not so, Lord! For I have never eaten anything common or unclean." 15 And a voice spoke to him again the second time, "What God has cleansed you must not call common." 16 This was done three times. And the object was taken up into heaven again.

Example: John's Vision in Revelation

The Book of Revelation begins with the Apostle John experiencing an open vision, which then progresses into a trance-starting in Revelation chapter 4.

Revelation 4:1–2
After these things I looked, and behold, a door standing open in heaven. And the first voice which I heard was like a trumpet speaking with me, saying, "Come up here, and I will show you things which must take place after this." 2 Immediately I was in the Spirit; and behold, a throne set in heaven, and One sat on the throne.

Prayer

Father, in the name of Jesus, let everything blinding my eyes, deafening my ears, and closing my heart and that of every reader to your communications via visions and dreams be roasted by fire now. Let there be a fresh outpouring of your Spirit upon me, my family, and every reader, so that we may prophesy, dream dreams, and see visions in the name of Jesus. Psalm 119:18; Joel 2:28

Chapter 9

How God Speaks: Types of Dreams

Ecclesiastes 5:7
For in the multitude of dreams and many words there is also vanity. But fear God.

God speaks through dreams, but not every dream carries divine significance. In this chapter, we will examine the **four main types of dreams** and learn how to discern which are meaningful and which are not.

1. The Perfect Dream

In a **perfect dream**, everything is clear, direct, and without symbolism. There are **no parables, no figures, no mystery**, and **no interpretation is needed**. What you see in the dream is **exactly what happens in real life**. These are rare but powerful.

Examples of Perfect Dreams:

Joseph's Dream (about Mary)

Matthew 1:20–24
But while he thought about these things, behold, an angel of the Lord appeared to him in a dream, saying, "Joseph, son of David, do not be afraid to take to you Mary your wife, for

that which is conceived in her is of the Holy Spirit. 21 And
she will bring forth a Son, and you shall call His name
Jesus, for He will save His people from their sins." 22 So all
this was done that it might be fulfilled which was spoken by
the Lord through the prophet, saying: 23 "Behold, the virgin
shall be with child, and bear a Son, and they shall call His
name Immanuel," which is translated, "God with us." 24
Then Joseph, being aroused from sleep, did as the angel of
the Lord commanded him and took to him his wife.

Joseph's Dream (Flight to Egypt)

Matthew 2:13–15
*Now when they had departed, behold, an angel of the Lord
appeared to Joseph in a dream, saying, "Arise, take the
young Child and His mother, flee to Egypt, and stay there
until I bring you word; for Herod will seek the young Child
to destroy Him."*
*14 When he arose, he took the young Child and His mother
by night and departed for Egypt, 15 and was there until the
death of Herod, that it might be fulfilled which was spoken
by the Lord through the prophet, saying, "Out of Egypt I
called My Son."*

Abimelech's Dream

Genesis 20:3–7
*But God came to Abimelech in a dream by night, and said to
him, "Indeed you are a dead man because of the woman
whom you have taken, for she is a man's wife." 4 But
Abimelech had not come near her; and he said, "Lord, will
You slay a righteous nation also? 5 Did he not say to me,*

'She is my sister'? And she, even she herself said, 'He is my brother.' In the integrity of my heart and innocence of my hands I have done this."

6 And God said to him in a dream, "Yes, I know that you did this in the integrity of your heart. For I also withheld you from sinning against Me; therefore I did not let you touch her.

7 Now therefore, restore the man's wife; for he is a prophet, and he will pray for you and you shall live. But if you do not restore her, know that you shall surely die, you and all who are yours."

Solomon's Dream (Granting of Wisdom)

1 Kings 3:11–15

Then God said to him: "Because you have asked this thing, and have not asked long life for yourself, nor have asked riches for yourself, nor have asked the life of your enemies, but have asked for yourself understanding to discern justice, 12 behold, I have done according to your words; see, I have given you a wise and understanding heart, so that there has not been anyone like you before you, nor shall any like you arise after you. 13 And I have also given you what you have not asked: both riches and honor, so that there shall not be anyone like you among the kings all your days. 14 So if you walk in My ways, to keep My statutes and My commandments, as your father David walked, then I will lengthen your days." 15 Then Solomon awoke; and indeed it had been a dream. And he came to Jerusalem and stood before the ark of the covenant of the Lord, offered up burnt offerings, offered peace offerings, and made a feast for all his servants.

2. Parable Dreams

Parable dreams are the **most common type of dreams**. They are **figurative, symbolic, and coded**. In these dreams, you might see trees talking, strange creatures, or symbolic actions. These dreams **require interpretation**.

Examples of Parable Dreams:

Joseph's Dream (Sheaves and Stars)

Genesis 37:6–9
So he said to them, "Please hear this dream which I have dreamed: 7 There we were, binding sheaves in the field. Then behold, my sheaf arose and also stood upright; and indeed your sheaves stood all around and bowed down to my sheaf." 8 And his brothers said to him, "Shall you indeed reign over us? Or shall you indeed have dominion over us?" So they hated him even more for his dreams and for his words. 9 Then he dreamed still another dream and told it to his brothers, and said, "Look, I have dreamed another dream. And this time, the sun, the moon, and the eleven stars bowed down to me."

Butler and Baker's Dreams

Genesis 40:9–11
Then the chief butler told his dream to Joseph, and said to him, "Behold, in my dream a vine was before me, 10 and in

the vine were three branches; it was as though it budded, its blossoms shot forth, and its clusters brought forth ripe grapes. 11 Then Pharaoh's cup was in my hand; and I took the grapes and pressed them into Pharaoh's cup, and placed the cup in Pharaoh's hand."

Genesis 40:16–17
When the chief baker saw that the interpretation was good, he said to Joseph, "I also was in my dream, and there were three white baskets on my head. 17 In the uppermost basket were all kinds of baked goods for Pharaoh, and the birds ate them out of the basket on my head."

Pharaoh's Dream (Cows and Grain)

Genesis 41:1–7
Then it came to pass, at the end of two full years, that Pharaoh had a dream; and behold, he stood by the river. 2 Suddenly there came up out of the river seven cows, fine looking and fat; and they fed in the meadow. 3 Then behold, seven other cows came up after them out of the river, ugly and gaunt, and stood by the other cows on the bank of the river. 4 And the ugly and gaunt cows ate up the seven fine looking and fat cows. So Pharaoh awoke.
5 He slept and dreamed a second time; and suddenly seven heads of grain came up on one stalk, plump and good. 6 Then behold, seven thin heads, blighted by the east wind, sprang up after them.
7 And the seven thin heads devoured the seven plump and full heads. So Pharaoh awoke, and indeed, it was a dream.

Nebuchadnezzar's Dream (The Statue)

Daniel 2:31-35

"You, O king, were watching; and behold, a great image!
This great image, whose splendor was excellent, stood before
you; and its form was awesome. 32 This image's head was of
fine gold, its chest and arms of silver, its belly and thighs of
bronze, 33 its legs of iron, its feet partly of iron and partly of
clay. 34 You watched while a stone was cut out without
hands, which struck the image on its feet of iron and clay,
and broke them in pieces.
35 Then the iron, the clay, the bronze, the silver, and the
gold were crushed together, and became like chaff from the
summer threshing floors; the wind carried them away so
that no trace of them was found. And the stone that struck
the image became a great mountain and filled the whole
earth.

When Should You Take a Parable Dream Seriously?

You should pay close attention to a symbolic or
parable-like dream when the following occur:

I. When You Remember It Clearly
If the dream remains vivid and detailed after waking,
it's likely more than just a passing thought. God often
ensures we remember what He wants us to reflect on
and respond to.

II. When You Wake Up Disturbed in Your Spirit
A deep inner disturbance can be a spiritual indicator
that the dream carries weight. Pharaoh experienced
this after his dream in Genesis 41:8:

"His spirit was troubled, and he sent and called for all the magicians of Egypt... but there was no one who could interpret the dream."

Nebuchadnezzar had a similar experience in Daniel 2:1: *"His spirit was so troubled that his sleep left him."*

When your spirit is unsettled after a dream, don't dismiss it—seek the Holy Spirit for clarity.

III. **When the Dream Is Repeated in a Short Span of Time**
Repeated dreams are often a divine emphasis. In Genesis 41:32, Joseph explained to Pharaoh:

"The dream was repeated... because the thing is established by God, and God will shortly bring it to pass."

A repeated dream signals urgency and certainty—it's a message that must not be ignored.

In all cases, seek interpretation through prayer and the Holy Spirit. The weight of a dream is not just in its symbolism, but in the spiritual prompting that comes with it.

3. Business Dreams

These are dreams that result from **daily activities**, mental overload, or busyness. They are **meaningless**

replays of daily life distorted with random twists and exaggerations

Ecclesiastes 5:3
For a dream comes through much activity, And a fool's voice is known by his many words.

These dreams usually carry little to no spiritual significance and should not be taken seriously.

4. Nightmares or Terrifying Dreams

These are **disturbing and frightening dreams,** often **demonically inspired,** designed to instill **fear and exert spiritual manipulation.** Their purpose is to unsettle your spirit and open the door to fear-based bondage.

Job 7:14
Then You scare me with dreams And terrify me with visions,

Job accused God of terrifying him with dreams, when in reality it was the devil behind the torment. Job didn't realize that, although God allowed the affliction, it was the enemy carrying it out.

Similarly, some nightmares stem not from spiritual sources but from natural ones or media influences — like horror movies you've watched or deep-seated fears that dominate your thoughts.

Regardless of the source, remember this: we are not governed by dreams—we are governed by the Word of God. No matter what the dream may reveal, it can be overturned, canceled, and redefined by standing on God's Word.

Prayer

Father, in the name of Jesus, by the operation of the Holy Spirit, help me and every reader to discern between dreams that are vital to our destiny and those that are not. Grant us grace to understand and respond appropriately to the important dreams, and help us to recognize your voice through dreams and visions, in Jesus' name.
Job 33:14–17; Numbers 12:6

Chapter 10

Keys to Interpreting Dreams and Visions

Daniel 1:17
As for these four young men, God gave them knowledge and skill in all literature and wisdom; and Daniel had understanding in all visions and dreams.

1. Only the Holy Spirit Can Interpret Dreams

Dreams are **divine communications**, and only **God Himself** can accurately interpret them through the **Holy Spirit**. Anyone who claims to interpret dreams **without the help of the Holy Spirit** is not speaking by God's authority.

Joseph affirmed this truth when the butler and baker sought someone to interpret their dreams, reminding them that interpretation belongs to God.

Genesis 40:8
And they said to him, "We each have had a dream, and there is no interpreter of it." So Joseph said to them, "Do not interpretations belong to God? Tell them to me, please."

Joseph repeated this when Pharaoh was unable to find anyone in his kingdom to interpret his dream. When Joseph was brought before him, he again made it clear that interpretation belongs to God.

Genesis 41:15–16
And Pharaoh said to Joseph, "I have had a dream, and there is no one who can interpret it. But I have heard it said of you that you can understand a dream, to interpret it." 16 So Joseph answered Pharaoh, saying, "It is not in me; God will give Pharaoh an answer of peace."

Daniel echoed the same truth when he interpreted King Nebuchadnezzar's dream. He acknowledged that only God could reveal and interpret the mystery, ultimately saving all the wise men from the king's wrath.

Daniel 2:26–28
The king answered and said to Daniel, whose name was Belteshazzar, "Are you able to make known to me the dream which I have seen, and its interpretation?" 27 Daniel answered in the presence of the king, and said, "The secret which the king has demanded, the wise men, the astrologers, the magicians, and the soothsayers cannot declare to the king. 28 But there is a God in heaven who reveals secrets, and He has made known to King Nebuchadnezzar what will be in the latter days. Your dream, and the visions of your head upon your bed, were these:"

Insight:

This means that anyone claiming to interpret dreams apart from the Holy Spirit is misleading you. True interpretation comes only by the Spirit of God. Dream interpretation books that rely solely on symbols or human reasoning are flawed — unless they acknowledge that understanding dreams requires the guidance of the Holy Spirit.

King Nebuchadnezzar understood this well. He knew that the so-called wise men and psychics of his day could fabricate interpretations, which is why he demanded they first tell him the dream itself before he would trust anything they said.

2. Apply Scriptural Rules or Patterns for Interpretation

There are **biblical patterns** or **rules** that can guide dream interpretation, but they must still be **applied under the direction of the Holy Spirit.**

Repeated Dreams

Genesis 41:32
And the dream was repeated to Pharaoh twice because the thing is established by God, and God will shortly bring it to pass.

When a dream is repeated—whether in the same form or in different variations—it often signifies that the matter has been established by God and is set to come to pass. However, before applying this principle, you must first be sure that the dream is truly from God and not simply a product of mental overload (a business dream) or a demonic, fear-driven manipulation.

If Scripture shows that some dreams cannot be changed, it also implies that others can. No dream is absolute. Every dream can be challenged, canceled, or reversed through the Word of God and prayer.

In cases where a dream cannot be changed, it is usually a divine warning—not a verdict. Its purpose is to prompt a response, so the negative outcome can be avoided, just like Pharaoh's dream in Genesis, which was a call to prepare, not to panic.

Specific Numbers Refer to Time

Another scriptural principle for interpreting dreams comes from the three dreams Joseph interpreted. When a dream includes a specific number of objects or elements that leave a strong impression—such as three cars, four mangoes, or seven doors—it often points to a time frame: days, months, or years.

This pattern is evident in Joseph's interpretations, where the number of items in the dream corresponded directly to periods of time. Let's look at a few examples from those dreams to see how this principle applies.

Butler's Dream

Genesis 40:9–11
Then the chief butler told his dream to Joseph, and said to him, "Behold, in my dream a vine was before me, 10 and in the vine were three branches; it was as though it budded, its blossoms shot forth, and its clusters brought forth ripe grapes. 11 Then Pharaoh's cup was in my hand; and I took the grapes and pressed them into Pharaoh's cup, and placed the cup in Pharaoh's hand."

In the butler's dream, he saw a vine with **three branches** that blossomed and produced grapes. He took the grapes and pressed them into Pharaoh's cup. Joseph interpreted this to mean that **within three days**, the butler would be restored to his position of service before Pharaoh.

Baker's Dream

Genesis 40:16–17
When the chief baker saw that the interpretation was good, he said to Joseph, "I also was in my dream, and there were three white baskets on my head. 17 In the uppermost basket were all kinds of baked goods for Pharaoh, and the birds ate them out of the basket on my head."

In the baker's dream, he saw **three baskets on his head**, with the top basket filled with all kinds of baked goods for Pharaoh. But birds came and ate the food out of the basket. Joseph interpreted **the three baskets to represent three days,** after which Pharaoh would have the baker executed, and his body left exposed for the birds to consume

Pharaoh's Dream

Genesis 41:1–7
Then it came to pass, at the end of two full years, that Pharaoh had a dream; and behold, he stood by the river. 2 Suddenly there came up out of the river seven cows, fine looking and fat; and they fed in the meadow. 3 Then behold, seven other cows came up after them out of the river, ugly and gaunt... 5 He slept and dreamed a second time; and suddenly seven heads of grain came up on one stalk, plump and good... 7 And the seven thin heads devoured the seven plump and full heads. So Pharaoh awoke, and indeed, it was a dream.

In Pharaoh's dream, there were **seven fat cows** followed by **seven thin and ugly cows,** as well as **seven healthy heads of grain** followed by **seven withered ones**. Joseph interpreted these to represent **seven years of abundance** followed by **seven years of famine.**

The key question is this: how do you know whether the numbers in a dream represent days, months, or years? That's a question only the Holy Spirit can answer. This is why, when you receive a symbolic or parable-like dream, you must pray and ask the Holy Spirit for interpretation.

There have been times when I didn't understand a dream right away. But after praying, God gave me another dream that unlocked the meaning of the first. Interpretation belongs to God, and He reveals it to those who seek Him.

3. Apply Scriptural Symbolism

The **Bible provides figurative meanings** for many objects and animals in dreams.

Trees = People

Psalm 1:3
He shall be like a tree planted by the rivers of water, That brings forth its fruit in its season...

Isaiah 61:3
That they may be called trees of righteousness, The planting of the Lord...

King Nebuchadnezzar was referred to as a tree in Dan.4:20

Daniel 4:20–22
"The tree that you saw, which grew and became strong... 22 it is you, O king...

The two witnesses in Revelation are described as olive trees.

Revelation 11:3–4
And I will give power to my two witnesses... 4 These are the two olive trees...

Horns = Power or Authority or Kings. Zechariah 1:18-21; Daniel 7:19-25; 8:19-20; Revelation 13:1;

Daniel 8:19–20
...Look, I am making known to you what shall happen... 20 The ram which you saw, having the two horns — they are the kings of Media and Persia.

Beasts = Kingdoms or Powers

Daniel 8:19–20 also references beasts as **nations or ruling powers**.

Mountains = Obstacles or Glory. Zechariah 4:7; Mark 11:23;

Zechariah 4:7
Who are you, O great mountain? Before Zerubbabel you shall become a plain!

Seas = Obstacles, Peoples, Nations, Sustenance. Daniel 7:1-28; Revelation 13:1-9; Psalms 114:1-3;

Psalm 114:1–3
*When Israel went out of Egypt... 3 The sea saw it and fled;
Jordan turned back.*

Snakes = Satan, Deception, Witchcraft, Demons

Genesis 3:13
The serpent deceived me, and I ate.

Luke 10:19
Behold, I give unto you power to tread on serpents...

Revelation 12:9
...that serpent of old, called the Devil and Satan...

4. Apply Natural Characteristics

Many dreams can be interpreted using the **natural
traits of animals or objects**.

Take the tortoise, for example. Its most obvious
characteristics are its slow pace and hard shell. So, if
you see a tortoise in a dream, it often symbolizes
delay, sluggish progress, or resistance. The same
applies to a snail—both point to slowness or
hindrance.

Now consider rats and cockroaches. These creatures
are known for being sneaky and destructive. Seeing
them in a dream can indicate hidden or subtle
destruction, loss, or devouring forces at work in your

life. They often symbolize devourers or spiritual thieves.

A car or vehicle, on the other hand, generally represents movement, speed, status, power, or help. The context of the dream is key. If you're driving, it may symbolize control, direction, or authority. If someone else is driving you, it could mean assistance — or possibly a loss of control. A dream of acceleration might point to promotion or divine momentum.

These are just a few examples, and we could explore many more symbols. But it's essential to interpret every dream under the guidance of the Holy Spirit. Symbols alone are not enough — their meaning is always subject to context and divine insight.

5. Personal Peculiarities in Interpretation

Every dream — and its interpretation — is deeply personal.

Dreams are not one-size-fits-all. While there are general principles drawn from Scripture and nature that can guide interpretation, every dream must be understood in light of the individual's unique values, experiences, and emotional associations. These personal elements are key ingredients in unlocking the true meaning of a dream or vision.

Personal Symbols in Relationships

Certain family members or friends may carry specific emotional weight or meaning in your life. Some may represent comfort, encouragement, or safety. Others might represent criticism, conflict, discouragement, or even malice. When God uses their faces or presence in a dream, He is often communicating something about what they symbolize to you — not necessarily about the person themselves. The message is tied to what they represent in your inner world.

Unique Personal Associations

Dreams also draw on your personal likes, dislikes, and sensitivities. For example, if you are considering entering a business or relationship with someone, and in a dream you find yourself eating food you're allergic to or strongly dislike — with that person — this could be a warning. It may be God's way of telling you that the connection is not safe or healthy.

However, that same dream might mean something entirely different for someone else, depending on their own experiences and associations. That's why even if two people have similar dreams, their interpretations could differ based on their individual contexts.

Ultimately, every dream must be interpreted prayerfully, with the help of the Holy Spirit, and in light of your unique journey

6. Conclusion

- All interpretation principles must be applied under the guidance of the Holy Spirit. Without Him, understanding is limited and potentially misleading.

- You cannot begin to understand or interpret your dreams unless you first take them seriously. Dismissing them robs you of insight and direction.

- No matter how serious a dream may seem, its outcome can be altered through prayer, the Word of God, and by responding to any warning it contains. Dreams are not final verdicts — they are often divine invitations to act.

- Ultimately, you are the best person to interpret your dreams. God often uses the language of your own life — your symbols, emotions, and experiences — to speak to you. Seek the Holy Spirit's help, and trust Him to unfold the meaning.

Prayer

Father, in the name of Jesus, grant me and every reader the wisdom and skill to understand and interpret our dreams and visions accurately, and to be guided by the revelation contained in them, in Jesus'

name.
Daniel 1:17; Daniel 9:22

Chapter 11

How God Speaks: Circumstances

Genesis 45:4–8
4 And Joseph said to his brothers, "Please come near to me." So they came near. Then he said: "I am Joseph your brother, whom you sold into Egypt. 5 But now, do not therefore be grieved or angry with yourselves because you sold me here; for God sent me before you to preserve life. 6 For these two years the famine has been in the land, and there are still five years in which there will be neither plowing nor harvesting. 7 And God sent me before you to preserve a posterity for you in the earth, and to save your lives by a great deliverance. 8 So now it was not you who sent me here, but God; and He has made me a father to Pharaoh, and lord of all his house, and a ruler throughout all the land of Egypt."

Introduction

God often uses circumstances to get our attention and guide our decisions. According to Job 33:14–24, this is typically one of the last ways He chooses to speak. God's preferred method is to speak directly — through the inner voice, spiritual impressions, or dreams and visions. But when those are ignored or misunderstood, He begins to move through external situations.

By the time God is speaking to you through circumstances, it's likely He has already been trying to reach you in other ways — and you didn't respond.

For example, He may have been prompting you to leave a job or end a relationship through inner conviction or repeated dreams. When you fail to discern it, He might allow you to be fired unexpectedly or cause that relationship to break down — not to harm you, but to reposition you for something better.

Circumstantial guidance can be uncomfortable — even painful — but it is often redemptive. It's not God's first choice, but He will use it if that's what it takes to realign you with His will.

Bottom line: Don't wait for God to speak through painful circumstances. Train your spirit to hear Him early — when He speaks gently.

Why God Uses Circumstances to Communicate

While circumstances are often a last resort when we ignore God's inner voice, they remain one of the most important ways He communicates with us — for several key reasons

1. God Uses Circumstances to Communicate What We're Not Yet Ready to Hear

There are things God wants to say, but we're simply not ready to receive them. So, He lets us live through experiences that teach us what words alone cannot.

John 16:12-13
"I still have many things to say to you, but you cannot bear them now. However, when He, the Spirit of truth, has come, He will guide you into all truth…"

Some lessons require a journey, not just a word.

Take Joseph, for example. If God had shown him the betrayal, slavery, and imprisonment he would endure before becoming prime minister of Egypt, he might never have shared his dreams with such boldness — or embraced the path at all. God often shows us the glory but withholds the process, knowing we might resist the calling if we knew the cost.

God Uses Circumstances to Shield Us From What We're Not Ready to Face

When God brought Israel out of Egypt, He deliberately avoided the shortest route:

Exodus 13:17
"He did not lead them through the land of the Philistines,

though that was near; for God said, 'Lest perhaps the people change their minds when they see war, and return to Egypt.'"

God was guiding them with wisdom. Though it seemed indirect, the detour was strategic. Circumstances often redirect us away from battles we're not yet equipped to fight.

Circumstances Reveal What Calling Doesn't Always Disclose

Jeremiah struggled with this reality. God called him, but didn't fully reveal the weight of that calling upfront: Jeremiah felt blindsided—not because God lied, but because the full reality of the assignment was only unveiled through the journey.

Jeremiah 20:7–8 (NIV)
"You deceived me, Lord, and I was deceived; you overpowered me and prevailed. I am ridiculed all day long; everyone mocks me... So the word of the Lord has brought me insult and reproach all day long."

2. God Uses Circumstances to Build Character

God often shapes His servants in the crucible of adversity. He uses challenging circumstances as tools for transformation, refining our hearts and developing spiritual maturity.

Affliction as a Teacher
The psalmist recognized this truth when he said:

Psalm 119:71
"It is good for me that I have been afflicted, that I may learn Your statutes."

Hardship becomes a classroom where God imparts deep spiritual lessons that comfort and ease could never teach.

Trials as Character Builders
James echoes this principle:

James 1:2–4
"Count it all joy when you fall into various trials, knowing that the testing of your faith produces patience. But let patience have its perfect work, that you may be perfect and complete, lacking nothing."

Trials are not punishments — they are tools. God uses them to produce patience, maturity, and depth in us.

The Prodigal Son as an Example
The turning point in the life of the prodigal son came through hardship. When he hit rock bottom, his attitude changed.

Luke 15:17–19
"But when he came to himself, he said, 'How many of my father's hired servants have bread enough and to spare, and

I perish with hunger! I will arise and go to my father and say to him, "Father, I have sinned..."'"

Desperation led to revelation. It was adversity that brought him back to his senses — and back to the Father.

Even Jesus Was Shaped by Suffering
Though perfect, Jesus modeled this principle in His own life:

Hebrews 5:8
"Though He was a Son, yet He learned obedience by the things which He suffered."

If Jesus — being the Son of God — was trained through suffering, how much more will God use difficult circumstances to train us?

God uses circumstances not just to speak, but to shape. When words alone won't work, He lets life speak. And often, it's in the furnace of real experiences that we gain wisdom, clarity, and depth. Instead of resisting circumstances, ask God, "What are You showing me through this?" His hand is often present — even when His voice seems silent

3. God Uses Circumstances to Reveal You to Yourself

One of the most profound functions of divinely orchestrated circumstances is self-revelation. God allows us to walk through situations not just to change our environment, but to expose what lies within us.

Your Response Reveals Your Condition

How you respond under pressure reveals the true state of your heart—your strengths, weaknesses, convictions, and character. God led the Israelites through the wilderness not just to deliver them from Egypt, but to reveal what was in their hearts.

Deuteronomy 8:2–3

"And you shall remember that the Lord your God led you all the way these forty years in the wilderness, to humble you and test you, to know what was in your heart, whether you would keep His commandments or not. So He humbled you, allowed you to hunger, and fed you with manna… that He might make you know that man shall not live by bread alone, but by every word that proceeds from the mouth of the Lord."

The wilderness exposed their inner reality—and it does the same for us.

Pressure Exposes True Character

True character is never revealed in comfort. It's under pressure that we truly see ourselves. Peter believed he would never deny Jesus, but under the heat of fear and pressure, he denied Him three times in just a few hours (John 13:36–38; 18:15–27).

Ruth's resilience and loyalty were revealed only after she lost her husband and father-in-law. Her famous declaration to Naomi came in the face of grief and uncertainty:

Ruth 1:16–17
"Where you go, I will go… your people shall be my people, and your God, my God."

The Purpose of Revelation Is Transformation
God doesn't expose you to shame you—He reveals you to heal you. The purpose of self-revelation is to help you see who you really are so you can align with who you are called, created, and destined to become.

Until you truly see yourself, you cannot change. And God, in His mercy, uses circumstances to help you do just that.

4. God Uses Circumstances to Direct You

Sometimes, God redirects our paths by closing certain doors and opening others. What may look like a setback or an unexpected turn is often divine navigation.

Paul's Open Door in Ephesus
Paul chose to remain in Ephesus because God had orchestrated circumstances that created a significant opportunity for ministry.

1 Corinthians 16:8–9
"But I will tarry in Ephesus until Pentecost. For a great and effective door has opened to me, and there are many adversaries."

An open door from God is not always free of challenges. In fact, the presence of opposition often confirms the significance of the opportunity.

Paul's Closed Doors in Asia and Bithynia
At other times, Paul's missionary plans were halted because the Holy Spirit redirected him.

Acts 16:6–7
"They were forbidden by the Holy Spirit to preach the word in Asia… they tried to go into Bithynia, but the Spirit did not permit them."

Closed doors can be as much divine direction as open ones. God doesn't just guide us by saying "Go" — He also leads us by saying "No."

Joseph's Life: Directed by Orchestrated Circumstances
God spoke to Joseph through dreams in his youth, but the actual path to his destiny unfolded through a series of divinely engineered events.

Genesis 45:4–8
"I am Joseph your brother, whom you sold into Egypt. But now, do not… be grieved or angry with yourselves because

you sold me here; for God sent me before you to preserve life… So now it was not you who sent me here, but God."

From being sold into slavery, to serving in Potiphar's house, to being falsely accused and imprisoned, and finally rising to become prime minister of Egypt — every step was guided by God's hand.

What his brothers meant for evil, God turned into a strategic positioning to save lives. Joseph could have chosen bitterness, but instead he recognized the divine orchestration behind his journey.

When he said, *"It was not you who sent me here, but God,"* he was acknowledging that even through human wrongdoing, God was steering the course of his life toward His intended purpose.

God's Plan May Use Painful Circumstances for Good

At first glance, Joseph's story raises a challenging question: Did God do evil by allowing a 17-year-old boy to be hated and sold by his brothers? Can God do evil?

The answer is no — God cannot do evil. But He can permit events that seem unjust in the moment because He knows the end from the beginning. At the time,

Joseph's situation appeared to be pure misfortune. Yet with the benefit of hindsight, we see that it was all part of God's redemptive plan.

Joseph himself acknowledged this when he told his brothers:

Genesis 50:20
"As for you, you meant evil against me; but God meant it for good, in order to bring it about as it is this day, to save many people alive."

This means that the painful events you've experienced—rejection, betrayal, disappointment, resistance, job loss, bereavement, or seasons of intense hardship—may not be "bad" in the ultimate sense. It's not the hardship itself that defines the outcome; it's God's intention and purpose in allowing it.

When God engineers or permits seemingly negative circumstances, it is never to destroy you—it is always to accomplish something good. So, when He says, "I have a plan to prosper you, to give you a future and a hope," (Jeremiah 29:11) and soon after everything seems to be falling apart, you must trust that even the chaos is part of the plan.

God may slam certain doors shut, allow people to step on you, or even permit you to be dragged into difficult situations—not because He has abandoned you, but because He is positioning you for a greater purpose.

Sometimes, it's not the devil. It's God. He may even allow the enemy to believe he's winning, as in Job's case, when in reality, God is orchestrating everything for your good.

I recall prophesying to a young lady that she was about to be promoted at her job. The very next week, she was suspended. Confused, she called me: "Pastor, you said I would be promoted, but I've just been suspended. Did I hear you wrong?" I reassured her that God was still in control and that it would turn out for her good.

Sure enough, when the suspension ended, she was promoted immediately. The suspension had come from a false accusation, which prompted management to examine her work more closely — only to discover that she had been undervalued and deserved promotion. What seemed like a setback was actually God's setup.

Lessons to Remember

- God's purposes can hide inside painful events — what looks like loss may be the very tool God uses to position you for gain.
- It's not the event, but God's intention that defines its value — the same situation meant for harm can be used by God for good.

- Trust God's plan when life doesn't make sense — delays, rejections, and even accusations can be part of the road to your promotion or breakthrough.

Stop Fighting What God is Using

God engineers circumstances for His purposes. Yet, because we often fail to recognize His hand in them, we react in frustration—jumping from place to place, blaming God like Job did, and exhausting ourselves emotionally.

James offers a different perspective:

James 1:2–4
"My brethren, count it all joy when you fall into various trials, knowing that the testing of your faith produces patience. But let patience have its perfect work, that you may be perfect and complete, lacking nothing."

Even when your circumstances arise from your own mistakes or from the enemy's attacks, God can still weave them into His plan for your good. Paul reminds us:

Romans 8:28
"And we know that all things work together for good to those who love God, to those who are the called according to His purpose."

If you truly love the Lord and carry His calling, He can take even your worst missteps and turn them into steppingstones. With that understanding, you never have to live another day in regret or despair.

Think of Joseph and his eleven brothers — the first family of Israel. God permitted intense hatred to grow among them, leading to Joseph's betrayal. Years later, the one who had been betrayed stood before his brothers and told them not to be angry with themselves, because God had been behind it all, working toward a good purpose.

So why are you still bitter toward the friend who betrayed you, the relative who abandoned you, or the people who wronged you? Why do you still beat yourself up over past mistakes? Can't you see that God has been using even those painful events to shape your journey? You made certain choices, took certain turns, and gained priceless experience because of what happened. You are where you are today — partly because of those very moments you wish never happened.

I remember watching an interview on Larry King Live with the legendary actor Sidney Poitier. In a book he wrote for his daughter, he reflected on the choices that shaped him. Larry King asked, "Looking back, is there anything you would have done differently?" Sidney's answer was striking. He explained that every decision he made was so interconnected that removing even one could cause the whole chain to fall apart. Some decisions he once wished he hadn't made turned out to be necessary for him to become who he was. So he could not honestly say he had regrets.

Life works the same way for us. Some of the most critical decisions we make are forged in the corner where God has placed us—compelled by circumstances we would never have chosen.

When you understand this, you stop fighting the very process God is using to fulfill His purpose in you.

When God Won't Let You Stay Where You Are

Let's be honest—how many of us came to the Lord purely out of love for Him? I didn't. Most of us came because we had problems we couldn't solve, and in seeking answers, we found Him—and fell in love along the way.

This is one of the ways God works: He directs us by engineering our circumstances.

Philippians 2:13

"For it is God who works in you both to will and to do for His good pleasure."

That's why when life takes an unexpected turn, instead of panicking, we should pause and ask: Is God speaking to me through this? What is He saying here?

At some point in Joseph's journey, he realized that everything—his betrayal, his slavery, his imprisonment—was God's way of moving him into place for His purpose. That realization freed him to forgive his brothers.

Looking back at my own life, I can see that some of my biggest decisions came from recognizing God speaking through my circumstances. There were things I resisted until He brought me to a corner where I had no choice but to yield. My ministerial calling is one of them. Like Paul said:

1 Corinthians 9:16
"For if I preach the gospel, I have nothing to boast of, for necessity is laid upon me; yes, woe is me if I do not preach the gospel!"

God will keep influencing your path because He has a call on your life. You were predestined before the foundation of the world for specific assignments.

Ephesians 2:10
"For we are His workmanship, created in Christ Jesus for good works, which God prepared beforehand that we should walk in them."

He doesn't override your free will, but He will influence it. If you resist His leading, He may allow the very things you cling to—relationships, jobs, positions — to slip away, until you make the change He desires.

Proverbs 19:21
"There are many plans in a man's heart, nevertheless the Lord's counsel — that will stand."

Think of Jonah. God told him to preach in Nineveh. He boarded a ship in the opposite direction. God sent a storm, exposed him to the crew, and had him thrown overboard. Then He prepared a fish to swallow him until Jonah surrendered (Jonah 1–4). That's divine redirection through engineered circumstances.

When you see life through that lens, you stop wasting energy on hatred or bitterness toward those who hurt you. Many of the people who caused you pain were part of God's plan to move you forward.

Bishop T.D. Jakes once said he's grateful to the leaders who conspired to push him out of his small West Virginia church. If they hadn't, he never would have gone to Dallas and built The Potter's House into a global ministry. At the time, he wanted to fight, but God told him to leave. That "setback" was his setup for elevation.

Everything God does serves a good purpose. Everything He allows is designed to end in praise.

Colossians 3:3

"For you died, and your life is hidden with Christ in God."

If your life is hidden in Him, then anything that reaches you has already passed through His hands. That means it's not designed to destroy you—it's meant to shape you.

1 Corinthians 10:13
"No temptation has overtaken you except such as is common to man; but God is faithful, who will not allow you to be tempted beyond what you are able, but with the temptation will also make the way of escape, that you may be able to bear it."

Not every negative circumstance comes from God, but if it reaches you, He allowed it—and He can turn it for good. Not every positive circumstance is from Him either. The real question is: What's the intention behind it? God's intentions are always good. The enemy's intentions are always evil. And even when the circumstance comes from your own mistakes, if you love God and are called according to His purpose, He will work it for your good.

Principles for Recognizing God's Direction Through Circumstances

- **Open Doors May Come with Opposition**
  Don't assume resistance means the opportunity isn't

from God. Sometimes the enemy fights hardest at the entrance to your breakthrough.

- **Closed Doors Can Be Divine Protection**
  A "No" from God today may be the setup for a bigger "Yes" tomorrow. Paul wasn't permitted to go to certain regions because God had a different and better plan.
- **Patterns in Your Life Often Point to God's Hand**
  Like Joseph, when you look back, you may see how unrelated events and unexpected hardships were actually steps toward your destiny.
- **God Can Use Even the Actions of Others**
  Whether it's betrayal, rejection, or loss, God can turn human intent for evil into a tool for His good purpose.
- **Direction Often Comes Gradually**
  God rarely shows the full path at once. Instead, He leads you step-by-step, using situations to guide your decisions.

Prayer

Prayer
Father, in the name of Jesus, help me and every reader to recognize Your voice through each of our circumstances. Grant us grace to endure what we cannot change, change what we can, and the wisdom to know the difference in Jesus' name.
Genesis 45:4–8; James 1:5; Hebrews 4:16

CHAPTER 12

CIRCUMSTANCES: THE PATTERN OF THE EAGLE

Deuteronomy 32:11–13

As an eagle stirs up its nest, Hovers over its young, Spreading out its wings, taking them up, Carrying them on its wings, 12 So the Lord alone led him, And there was no foreign god with him. 13 "He made him ride in the heights of the earth, That he might eat the produce of the fields; He made him draw honey from the rock, And oil from the flinty rock."

God Leads by Engineering Circumstances

I n the last chapter, we learned that God speaks through circumstances. These are often the most important ways He leads us because there are things we may never receive, and moves we may never make, unless we are persuaded through situations He orchestrates.

It is God who works in us to will and to do for His good pleasure (Philippians 2:13). According to our anchor text, God led Israel the way an eagle leads its young.

How an Eagle Trains Its Young

1. **A High and Comfortable Nest** – The eagle builds its nest high on a mountain. It is woven with strong sticks and lined with grass, feathers, and other soft materials to make it cozy.
2. **Provision Until Maturity** – After the eaglets are born, the mother leaves them in the comfort of the nest and brings food daily until she believes they are developed enough to fly.
3. **Demonstrating Ability** – One day, she hovers over them, spreads her wings, and demonstrates what they are capable of. She repeats this several times, so they see they have what she has.
4. **Stirring the Nest** – Then, she begins tearing apart the cozy home. This is the meaning of *"As an eagle stirs up its nest"* — she dismantles their comfort until they are barely hanging on.
5. **Forcing the Leap** – She pushes them over the ledge. As they fall, she swoops down just before they hit the ground, lifts them high, and drops them again.
6. **Repeating Until They Try** – She does this over and over — five, six, or more times — until they finally attempt to spread their wings.
7. **The Breakthrough Flight** – Once they try, the wind lifts them, and they begin to glide. They discover they were created to fly all along.

God's Spiritual Process

Just like the eaglets, we can become too comfortable in our "nests." Our nature resists change because the unfamiliar feels uncertain. Most people only change when compelled by circumstances.

So, God shakes things:

- That boss you dislike shows up in your department.
- That job you thought you would retire from is taken away.
- That relationship you depended on ends.
- That friend or relative you trusted fails you.

Beloved, there is a shaking coming. The pandemic was one form of shaking, but there is another on the horizon. God is about to shake things that will move you to the place He has prepared for you, position you for your palace, and usher you into your next level in the name of Jesus.

Haggai 2:6–7 says:
"Once more (it is a little while) I will shake heaven and earth, the sea and dry land; and I will shake all nations, and they shall come to the Desire of All Nations, and I will fill this temple with glory," says the Lord of hosts.

Recognizing When You Must Act

When the eaglets realize they can't just wait for mother eagle to catch them, they conclude *I have to do something.*

This is where transformation happens:

- The **prodigal son** reached it and returned home (Luke 15:17–20).
- **Jabez** reached it and prayed for enlargement (1 Chronicles 4:10).
- **Jacob** reached it and wrestled until he was blessed (Genesis 32:24–30).

Until you take responsibility for your own destiny, you will keep falling. This is why some people's pastor's prayers "don't work" — not because the pastor is less anointed, but because the person refuses to act.

Learning to Spread Your Wings

The eaglets notice that before every drop, mother eagle spreads her wings. Eventually, they mimic her, spread their own wings, and the wind carries them.

This is a prophetic word: The wind of the Holy Spirit is ready to lift you — if you will leave your comfort zone. No sermon or laying on of hands could have made the eaglets fly; only engineered circumstances could.

God Can Build and Dismantle

Deuteronomy 32:39 says:
"Now see that I, even I, am He, And there is no God besides Me; I kill and I make alive; I wound and I heal; Nor is there any who can deliver from My hand."

God can give you a job today and take it tomorrow. He can build a business and remove it from your hands — not to harm you, but to grow you, push you to discover hidden capacities, and bring you to your glorious destiny in Christ.

Correcting Misconceptions

1. **Difficulty Does Not Always Mean You're Out of God's Will**
   - Paul said: *"A great and effective door has opened to me, and there are many adversaries"* (1 Corinthians 16:8–9).
   - In Matthew 14:22–32, the disciples obeyed Jesus' command to cross the sea but faced a storm.
   - In Mark 4:35–41, Jesus was in the boat with them when a violent storm arose.
2. **Ease Does Not Always Mean It's from God**
   - *"There is a way that seems right to a man, but its end is the way of death"* (Proverbs 14:12).
   - Wide gates lead to destruction (Matthew 7:13).

Three Key Questions When Facing Difficulty

1. **Am I to Endure or Change This Situation?**
   Some trials must be resisted and changed; others must be endured. Discernment is key.
2. **When Should I Stop Knocking on a Closed Door?**
   - Some persist in a place where God has moved on, holding on to careers, ministries, or businesses that God has already left.
   - Others quit too soon, abandoning what God intended them to press through.
3. **When Is God Changing My Focus?**
   - Like the eaglets, sometimes repeated "drops" mean God is forcing you to change strategy, focus, or location.

When to Stop Banging on the Door

1. **When Grace and Joy Are Gone**
   - 2 Corinthians 12:9: *"My grace is sufficient for you…"*
   - If God wants you to endure, He sends "reliefs" — moments of refreshing that strengthen you to keep going.
   - When grace lifts, joy dries up and everything becomes a struggle.
2. **When the Situation Damages Rather Than Builds Character**

- James 1:2–4 tells us trials are to develop character.
- Deuteronomy 8:2 says God tests us to humble us and reveal what is in our hearts.
- If the trial is making you cynical, bitter, or spiritually unhealthy, it may be time to change course.

3. **When God Will Not Intervene and the Burden Drains You Unnecessarily**
   - Sometimes, this doesn't mean abandoning the vision — but adjusting the method, location, or partners.
   - The eaglets eventually realized mother eagle would not stop dropping them. They had to change their response.

The Final Lesson

God sometimes engineers circumstances or closes doors to:

- Change your focus.
- Redirect your strategy.
- Transform your attitude.
- Reveal new aspects of Himself.

He is unchanging, but He provokes change in us so we can experience the full spectrum of who He is.

Prayer

Father, in the name of Jesus, let Your voice through my circumstances and that of every reader be clear enough to compel the **prompt and total obedience** of each one of us, so that **struggles will be terminated** in every area of our lives. Cause each of us to **mount up like the eagle and fly into our glorious destinies** this season in the name of Jesus.
Deuteronomy 32:11–13

CHAPTER 13

THE PATTERN OF GOD'S WILL

Why Understanding God's Will Matters

The purpose of learning how God speaks is so that we can understand His will for our lives — especially in the areas that are not explicitly written in the Word — and obtain divine direction.

In the previous chapters, we have studied how God communicates. In this chapter, we will examine "The Pattern of God's Will" so that we can have a more complete understanding of how to determine His will.

Ephesians 1:9–11

having made known to us the mystery of His will, according to His good pleasure which He purposed in Himself,
10 that in the dispensation of the fullness of the times He might gather together in one all things in Christ, both which are in heaven and which are on earth – in Him.
11 In Him also we have obtained an inheritance, being predestined according to the purpose of Him who works all things according to the counsel of His will.

Three Truths From Our Anchor Text

1. **God Has Revealed His Will** (v. 9) — The mystery of His will is not hidden from His children.
2. **The Ultimate Goal** (v. 10) — His plan is to gather everything in heaven and on earth together in Christ, where Christ will reign over all.
3. **God Works All Things According to His Will** (v. 11) — Every event and circumstance ultimately serves the fulfillment of His divine plan.

Basic Facts About the Will of God

1. God Wants You to Know His Will

- **The Bible Commands It** — *"Therefore do not be unwise, but understand what the will of the Lord is"* (Ephesians 5:17).
- **Paul Prayed for It** — *"…that you may be filled with the knowledge of His will in all wisdom and spiritual understanding"* (Colossians 1:9).
- **It Is Essential for Succes and Heaven** — *"Not everyone who says to Me, 'Lord, Lord,' shall enter… but he who does the will of My Father"* (Matthew 7:21).
- **It Requires Personal Pursuit** — Jesus said, *"…I do not seek My own will but the will of the Father who sent Me"* (John 5:30). We must *"seek first the kingdom of God"* (Matthew 6:33).

2. God's Will Is Planned

- **God's Will is Rooted in His Master Plan.** God is actively at work in the world, bringing everything into alignment with His divine plan:
  Ephesians 1:11
  In Him also we have obtained an inheritance, being predestined according to the purpose of Him who works all things according to the counsel of His will.
- **The Big Picture.** God has an overarching, universal design — what we can call His master plan. As we have seen earlier, that master plan is to unite all things, both in heaven and on earth, under the authority of Christ in the fullness of time:
  Ephesians 1:10
  That in the dispensation of the fullness of the times He might gather together in one all things in Christ, both which are in heaven and which are on earth – in Him.
- **An Individual Plan -** *Within that grand design, God also has a unique, personal plan for each individual. Each of us plays a role in fulfilling His overall purpose. For example, God said of Pharaoh:*
  Romans 9:17
  For the Scripture says to the Pharaoh, "For this very purpose I have raised you up, that I may show My power in you, and that My name may be declared in all the earth."

Just as Pharaoh's life was used to serve God's larger purposes, our lives are also woven into His eternal strategy.

3. God's Plan Is Personal

- **Redemption for All.** God's will for each person begins with His sovereign plan of redemption. His desire is that no one be lost, but that all would turn to Him in repentance and receive eternal life through faith in Christ:

  2 Peter 3:9
  The Lord is not slack concerning His promise, as some count slackness, but is longsuffering toward us, not willing that any should perish but that all should come to repentance.

  John 6:40
  And this is the will of Him who sent Me, that everyone who sees the Son and believes in Him may have everlasting life; and I will raise him up at the last day.

- **Unique Assignments.** Beyond redemption, God has a personal and unique plan for each individual — positioning us in specific places, at precise times, for purposes He has determined. Speaking of the prophet Jeremiah, God said:

  Jeremiah 1:5
  Before I formed you in the womb I knew you; Before you were born I sanctified you; I ordained you a prophet to the nations.

God's plans for each person are unique, which is why comparing your calling or assignment to someone else's is unwise. When Peter questioned Jesus about John's future, the Lord replied:
John 21:22

Jesus said to him, "If I will that he remain till I come, what is that to you? You follow Me."

Jesus had different missions for Peter and John, just as He has distinct plans for each of us.

- **Ordered Steps.** Not only does God have a plan, but He actively directs our steps toward fulfilling it. His guidance covers not just major life events, but the everyday steps that lead us to His desired end:
Psalm 37:23
The steps of a good man are ordered by the Lord, And He delights in his way.
Psalm 32:8
I will instruct you and teach you in the way you should go; I will guide you with My eye.

God's leading is both personal and precise — shaping the path before you, one step at a time.

4. God's Will Is Not Man's Way

- **God's Will Is Different from Man's Ways.** God's will often runs counter to human reasoning and natural inclinations. Our limited perspective cannot match His infinite wisdom and higher purposes:
Isaiah 55:8–9
"For My thoughts are not your thoughts, Nor are your ways My ways," says the Lord. 9 For as the heavens are higher than the earth, So are My ways higher than your ways, And My thoughts than your thoughts."
- **Because His ways are higher,** God's will is not always the path we would instinctively choose for

ourselves. This is why it is essential to learn to recognize and follow His voice. His leading may take you in directions that seem uncomfortable, unexpected, or even illogical at first. However, this does not mean His will is designed to make you miserable. On the contrary, His plans ultimately bring life, fulfillment, and joy — even if the route to get there challenges your preferences.

5. God's Will Is Good

- **By Nature.** God's will is not only perfect — it is inherently good. When you align with His purposes, you can trust that His plans are motivated by love and aimed at your ultimate benefit.
  Romans 12:2
  And do not be conformed to this world, but be transformed by the renewing of your mind, that you may prove what is that good and acceptable and perfect will of God.

- **By Intention** - His motives and intentions toward you are always good, never harmful.
  Jeremiah 29:11
  For I know the thoughts that I think toward you, says the Lord, thoughts of peace and not of evil, to give you a future and a hope.

- **By Outcome** — It fulfills His good pleasure. Even when His way differs from what you would naturally choose, you can rest assured that He knows what is truly best for you.

Ephesians 1:5
Having predestined us to adoption as sons by Jesus Christ to Himself, according to the good pleasure of His will.

6. God's Plan Is Progressive

- **Step By Step.** God's will for your life is not revealed all at once. Instead, He unfolds it step by step — *"line upon line, precept upon precept"* — shaping you over time into the person He has called you to be. You are a work in progress, continually being molded by His hand.
  Ephesians 2:10
  For we are His workmanship, created in Christ Jesus for good works, which God prepared beforehand that we should walk in them.

- **Ongoing** - God is not only the author of your life's plan; He is also the one actively bringing it to completion. This ongoing process involves both the inward shaping of your desires and the outward ordering of your steps.
  Philippians 2:13
  For it is God who works in you both to will and to do for His good pleasure.

  As long as you remain on this earth, you will be a work in progress — continually growing, learning, and being refined — until His perfect purpose is fully accomplished in you.

Two Main Divisions of God's Will

From our earlier studies, we can categorize the will of God into two broad divisions:

1. The Will of God Clearly Revealed in His Written Word

The Scriptures outline God's will in ways that are explicit and unchanging. Within this revealed will, there are three main dimensions:

- **The Sovereign Will (Boulēma Will of God)**
  These are events and purposes that will occur regardless of human cooperation or resistance. They form the broad outlines of God's master plan for the world and humanity. No man, system, or spiritual force can alter them.

- **The Individual Will (Thélēma Will of God)**
  This is God's specific plan for each person's life. While the sovereign will is fixed, the individual will requires your cooperation. It addresses the unique assignments, callings, and roles God has for you in His master plan.

- **The Moral Will of God**
  These are the commandments, principles, and instructions found in the Bible that show how God wants His children to live. They apply to all believers, regardless of time, culture, or circumstance.

- **Harmony of the Wills**
  God's individual will for your life will never

contradict His sovereign will or His moral will. They always align perfectly. Any "guidance" that conflicts with Scripture is not from God.

2. The Will of God Not Explicitly Revealed in His Written Word

There are many life decisions about which the Bible does not give direct, specific instructions — yet these decisions are important. Examples include:

- Your specific ministry or career path

- The church you should attend

- The person you should marry

- The city or nation where you should live

In these matters, you must seek God's direction and learn to recognize His voice.

Steps to Discerning God's Will in These Situations

i. **Search the Scriptures First**
Begin by studying the Word to see if there is specific guidance already provided. There is no need to "seek confirmation" when God has already spoken clearly in His Word.

ii. **Accept God's Word as His Voice to You**
If you reject the clear guidance of Scripture, you open yourself to deception.

iii. **Apply Biblical Principles**
Even when the Bible does not give a direct

command, it often provides general principles that, when understood and applied, will lead to a decision consistent with God's will.

Example of a General Principle
The Apostle Paul warns:

2 Corinthians 6:14-15
Do not be unequally yoked together with unbelievers. For what fellowship has righteousness with lawlessness? And what communion has light with darkness? 15 And what accord has Christ with Belial? Or what part has a believer with an unbeliever?

This principle — not being yoked with unbelievers — applies broadly:

- Marriage to an unbeliever

- Business partnerships with unbelievers

- Deep friendships that compromise your faith

Search for Biblical Biographies
Study the lives of men and women in Scripture who faced situations similar to yours. Observe the choices they made and whether those choices aligned with God's will.

When the Word Is Silent

In matters where Scripture does not provide direct guidance, we must depend on hearing God's voice through the means already discussed in this series — the inward witness, the peace of God, prophetic direction, and circumstances orchestrated by the Lord.

Romans 12:1-2
I beseech you therefore, brethren, by the mercies of God, that you present your bodies a living sacrifice, holy, acceptable to God, which is your reasonable service. 2 And do not be conformed to this world, but be transformed by the renewing of your mind, that you may prove what is that good and acceptable and perfect will of God.

This passage shows that to walk in the fullness of God's will — whether revealed in His Word or discerned through His Spirit — you must live in total surrender and continually renew your mind with His truth. To understand the pattern of God's Will we have to understand "What is meant by the good, acceptable, and perfect will of God?"

Understanding the Good, Acceptable, and Perfect Will of God
(Romans 12:1-2)

The Perfect Will of God
The perfect will of God is fulfilled when a believer's life is in complete harmony with:

1. **God's sovereign will** — His unchangeable master plan.
2. **God's moral will** — His commands and principles in Scripture.
3. **God's individual will** — His specific plan for that person's life.

This means:

- The believer has embraced God's sovereign plan of salvation through the new birth in Christ.
- They live in alignment with the moral commandments of God's Word.
- They have sought and discovered God's specific guidance for their individual life and are walking in it.
- Jesus Christ is the ultimate example of one who walked fully in the perfect will of God. He fulfilled every prophecy concerning Him and never deviated from the Father's plan.

The Good Will of God

When a believer is in the **good will of God**:

- They are not fully walking in God's perfect plan for their life, yet they remain within His sovereign will and moral will.
- They are not in direct disobedience to God's revealed Word.

- They are still actively seeking God's perfect will for their life but have not yet fully entered into it.

The Acceptable (Permissive) Will of God

In this realm:

- The believer is missing God's perfect will for their life but is still in an area God permits.
- They are living in what is sometimes called the *permissive will* of God.
- They may not even be concerned about discovering God's perfect will.
- God permits them to remain here, but it is not His best for them — and it can be dangerous.

Outside the Will of God

This is the most dangerous place to be:

- The believer (or professing believer) is in direct disobedience to God's sovereign, moral, and individual will.
- The question is; a believer who is in direct disobedience to God's sovereign, moral and individual will for his life is that still a believer? Jesus issued a sobering warning:

Matthew 7:21
"Not everyone who says to Me, 'Lord, Lord,' shall enter the

kingdom of heaven, but he who does the will of My Father in heaven."

An unbeliever is certainly outside the will of God. A professing believer who continually resists God's will may be in peril of self-deception.

Illustration from the Life of Balaam
(Numbers 22)

The story of Balaam demonstrates the progression from the **perfect will** of God into the **permissive will**, and the dangers that follow.

Balak, king of Moab, sent men to the prophet Balaam to hire him to curse Israel. God clearly told Balaam:

Numbers 22:12-13
And God said to Balaam, "You shall not go with them; you shall not curse the people, for they are blessed." 13 So Balaam rose in the morning and said to the princes of Balak, "Go back to your land, for the Lord has refused to give me permission to go with you."

This was God's **perfect will** — Balaam was not to go at all.

However, when Balak offered greater rewards, Balaam went back to God a second time seeking permission to go, even though he already knew God's will. God, seeing Balaam's greed, allowed him to go — a shift into the **permissive will**:

This is exactly what some believers do: even after God has revealed His perfect will, they keep returning to Him, asking for something different. In many cases, His perfect will is already made clear in the Scriptures, yet they continue to seek an alternative. In doing so, they expose themselves to deception, error, and unnecessary spiritual danger.

Numbers 22:20-21
And God came to Balaam at night and said to him, "If the men come to call you, rise and go with them; but only the word which I speak to you — that you shall do." 21 So Balaam rose in the morning, saddled his donkey, and went with the princes of Moab.

Immediately, Balaam was at risk.

Numbers 22:22
Then God's anger was aroused because he went, and the Angel of the Lord took His stand in the way as an adversary against him. And he was riding on his donkey, and his two servants were with him.

If not for the donkey's intervention, the angel would have killed him. Peter later described Balaam's heart:

2 Peter 2:15-16
They have forsaken the right way and gone astray, following the way of Balaam the son of Beor, who loved the wages of unrighteousness; 16 but he was rebuked for his iniquity: a dumb donkey speaking with a man's voice restrained the madness of the prophet.

Dangers of the Permissive Will of God

Walking in the permissive will is spiritually dangerous. Israel's wilderness history shows this:

Psalm 106:13-15
They soon forgot His works; They did not wait for His counsel,
14 But lusted exceedingly in the wilderness, And tested God in the desert. 15 And He gave them their request, But sent leanness into their soul.

Psalm 78:29-31
So they ate and were well filled, For He gave them their own desire. 30 They were not deprived of their craving; But while their food was still in their mouths, 31 The wrath of God came against them, And slew the stoutest of them, And struck down the choice men of Israel.

Like Balaam, Israel got what they insisted on — but at great cost. God granted their request—but it was outside His perfect will. Along with it came leanness of soul and the weight of His displeasure. He permitted their insistence, yet it provoked His wrath. Be careful what you press God to give you. The perfect will of God is the only place of absolute safety and assured success; anything outside of it is dangerous ground.

Other Biblical Examples

- **Abraham and Ishmael** — God promised a son through Sarah, but Abraham produced Ishmael through Hagar, stepping into the permissive will.
- **Moses and Aaron** — Aaron became spokesman because Moses resisted God's direct call to speak.

Pattern of a Believer's Conformity to the Perfect Will

1. **Jesus Christ** is the only person who walked in perfect, uninterrupted harmony with God's will.
2. **Most believers** experience an *up-and-down* walk — sometimes aligned with God's perfect will, other times missing it.
3. As long as they keep seeking God, even in a zigzag journey, they are still moving in the right direction.
4. Spiritual maturity narrows the deviations, bringing greater consistency in obedience.
5. Whether in the perfect, good, or acceptable will of God, **Romans 8:28** applies:

Romans 8:28
And we know that all things work together for good to those who love God, to those who are the called according to His purpose.

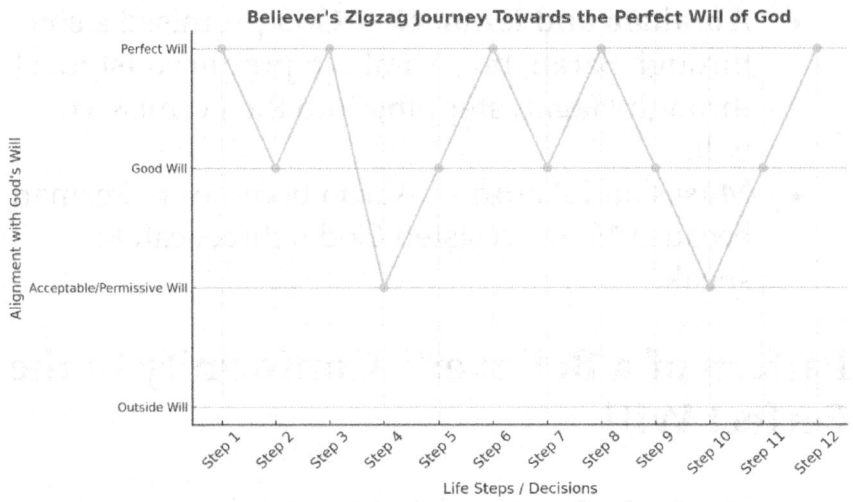

Believer's Zigzag Journey Towards the Perfect Will of God

Two Keys to Proving God's Will

Romans 12:1-2

I beseech you therefore, brethren, by the mercies of God, that you present your bodies a living sacrifice, holy, acceptable to God, which is your reasonable service. 2 And do not be conformed to this world, but be transformed by the renewing of your mind, that you may prove what is that good and acceptable and perfect will of God.

1. **Absolute Surrender** — Present your body as a living sacrifice.
2. **Renewed Mind** — Saturate it with God's Word.

Do these, and you will remain within His will.

PRAYERS

Prayer 1:

Father, in the name of Jesus, let Your will for my life, my family, and every reader be revealed step by step in ways that none of us will miss it. Let everything resisting the dominion of Your will in our lives be roasted by fire today. In Jesus' name. Amen.
Matt. 6:9-11; Eph. 5:17; Col. 1:9

Prayer 2:

Father, in the name of Jesus, let everything resisting my harmony with Your perfect will be eliminated today. Mold me, shape me, and bring me into conformity with Your perfect will and the image of Christ, in Jesus' name. Amen.
Romans 8:29-30

CHAPTER 14

WHAT DO YOU DO WHEN GOD IS SILENT

In previous chapters, we have been learning how to hear the voice of God — how He speaks in various ways. But what about those times when God does not speak? What happens when the heavens seem silent in that critical moment when you are in crisis and desperate to hear His direction so you can make the right decision?

Proverbs 3:5–6 reminds us:
Trust in the Lord with all your heart, And lean not on your own understanding; 6 In all your ways acknowledge Him, And He shall direct your paths.

Before we explore what to do when God is silent, we must first ask an important question: **Why would God be silent?** Are there seasons in a believer's life when heaven seems quiet? The answer is yes. Let's examine some of those seasons and the reasons behind them.

1. When You Are Not Listening
It is your attentiveness that provokes God's speaking. God has no reason to speak if you are not listening.

Proverbs 8:6 says:
Listen, for I will speak of excellent things, And from the opening of my lips will come right things.

If you are distracted or inattentive to God's voice, you will not hear Him.

Proverbs 7:24 emphasizes this:
Now therefore, listen to me, my children; Pay attention to the words of my mouth.

2. When You Are Under a Test

A teacher does not teach during an examination. You may be the teacher's favorite student, but on the day of the test, he is silent. His face may be expressionless, giving no clues. That's how it is with God during seasons of testing — He often doesn't speak until the test is over.

This was Job's frustration. In the most critical period of his life, when he needed God's voice the most, God was silent. Why? Because Job was under a test. God and Satan had agreed to test him (though Job was never told this).

God only spoke after Job had passed the test. Job himself held to this confidence:

Job 23:10
But He knows the way that I take; When He has tested me, I shall come forth as gold.

In other words, Job was saying: *I may not understand what's happening, I may not hear His voice, and what I'm going through may not make sense — but I trust Him. When this is over, it will work for my good.*

3. When You Are Going in the Right Direction

Most GPS systems remain silent when you are on the correct route. They only speak when you are about to make a wrong turn. Similarly, sometimes God's silence is an indication that you are on course. Keep moving forward until He speaks again.

Paul and Silas experienced this. They kept traveling until they were about to make a wrong move — then the Holy Spirit spoke.

Acts 16:6–7
Now when they had gone through Phrygia and the region of Galatia, they were forbidden by the Holy Spirit to preach the word in Asia. 7 After they had come to Mysia, they tried to go into Bithynia, but the Spirit did not permit them.

4. When You Haven't Obeyed the Last Instruction

God will not give you new instructions until you obey the last one He gave. His guidance is progressive — each word builds on the previous one.

Isaiah 28:13
But the word of the Lord was to them, "Precept upon

precept, precept upon precept, Line upon line, line upon line, Here a little, there a little..........."

Until you act on what God has already said—whether from His written Word or a personal directive—you are not ready for the next instruction.

5. When You Neglect His House
Neglecting the work of God and prioritizing your own affairs can close the heavens over your life.

Haggai 1:7–10
Thus says the Lord of hosts: "Consider your ways! 8 Go up to the mountains and bring wood and build the temple, that I may take pleasure in it and be glorified," says the Lord. 9 "You looked for much, but indeed it came to little; and when you brought it home, I blew it away. Why?" says the Lord of hosts. "Because of My house that is in ruins, while every one of you runs to his own house. 10 Therefore the heavens above you withhold the dew, and the earth withholds its fruit."

When God's house is neglected, His voice can become silent, and His blessings withheld

WHAT TO DO WHEN GOD IS SILENT:

Now that we know there are times when God may choose to be silent, what should you do in those moments?

What do you do when, like Job, you're facing devastating loss and heaven is quiet?
What do you do when you're confronting critical issues, need urgent direction, and yet God doesn't seem to answer?
What do you do when you've prayed, sown seeds, wept, and done all you know to do, yet the heavens feel like brass?

Here's how to respond when God is silent:

1. Trust in the Lord with All Your Heart

Proverbs 3:5–6
Trust in the Lord with all your heart, And lean not on your own understanding; 6 In all your ways acknowledge Him, And He shall direct your paths.

When God isn't speaking and the storms are raging, your first and most important posture is trust. Job expressed it this way:

Job 13:15
Though He slay me, yet will I trust Him. Even so, I will defend my own ways before Him.

It's easy to believe someone loves you when they constantly reassure you, meet your needs, and shower you with gifts. But trust is believing in that love even when all visible evidence disappears. Trust holds on when every signal says otherwise.

Job experienced unimaginable loss—children, wealth, health—yet he chose to trust God because he knew God had proven Himself faithful before.

Job 1:20–22
Then Job arose, tore his robe, and shaved his head; and he fell to the ground and worshiped. 21 And he said: "Naked I came from my mother's womb, And naked shall I return there. The Lord gave, and the Lord has taken away; Blessed be the name of the Lord." 22 In all this Job did not sin nor charge God with wrong.

The three Hebrew boys demonstrated the same trust before Nebuchadnezzar's fiery furnace:

Daniel 3:16–18
Shadrach, Meshach, and Abed-Nego answered and said to the king, "O Nebuchadnezzar, we have no need to answer you in this matter. 17 If that is the case, our God whom we serve is able to deliver us from the burning fiery furnace, and He will deliver us from your hand, O king. 18 But if not, let it be known to you, O king, that we do not serve your gods, nor will we worship the gold image which you have set up."

God Himself has demonstrated trust in you— entrusting you with life, His Word, His will, and even children, despite knowing your weaknesses and flaws.

He is looking for a people who will trust Him in both prosperity and adversity.

When it's dark and silent, trust Him—because God is in the silence, in the darkness, and in the unknown.

Isaiah 43:2
When you pass through the waters, I will be with you; And through the rivers, they shall not overflow you.
When you walk through the fire, you shall not be burned, Nor shall the flame scorch you.

Psalm 18:11
He made darkness His secret place; His canopy around Him was dark waters And thick clouds of the skies.

2. Lean Not on Your Own Understanding

Your understanding is limited, and in times of pain and confusion, it can be distorted by fear, trauma, and unstable emotions. Decisions made under such pressure are often poor ones.

Proverbs 3:5–6
Trust in the Lord with all your heart, And lean not on your own understanding; 6 In all your ways acknowledge Him, And He shall direct your paths.

Leaning on your own understanding may lead you to believe God has abandoned you—just as Gideon questioned when the angel greeted him:

Judges 6:12–13
And the Angel of the Lord appeared to him, and said to him, "The Lord is with you, you mighty man of valor!" 13 Gideon said to Him, "O my lord, if the Lord is with us, why then has all this happened to us? And where are all His miracles which our fathers told us about, saying, 'Did not the Lord bring us up from Egypt?' But now the Lord has forsaken us and delivered us into the hands of the Midianites."

Don't base your conclusion on what you see or feel. Anchor yourself to God's Word instead.

3. In All Your Ways Acknowledge Him
To acknowledge God is to keep honoring Him, even in silence. Don't stop praising. Don't stop worshiping. Don't withdraw from church, prayer, or obedience.

Job's response to loss was worship:

Job 1:20
Then Job arose, tore his robe, and shaved his head; and he fell to the ground and worshiped.

This is the time for deeper worship and louder praise. The enemy wants you discouraged, bitter, and silent toward God. If you respond that way, you fail the test. But if you worship through your pain, you provoke divine direction.

He may not speak audibly, but He will guide your steps. Without a dream or vision, you will find yourself making the right moves—not by accident, but because He is ordering your path.

He can turn wrong turns into blessings, close pits before you step in, or turn pitfalls into platforms. As long as you keep acknowledging Him, He will direct your path into peace, provision, and purpose.

FINAL THOUGHT

When heaven is silent, the temptation is to panic, withdraw, or take matters into your own hands. But silence is not absence, and delay is not denial. Trust anchors you when you cannot see the way. Refusing to lean on your own understanding keeps you from the traps of fear and faulty reasoning. Acknowledging Him in all your ways ensures that your worship becomes your compass, guiding you safely through uncharted waters.

In God's silence, He is still speaking—through His past faithfulness, through the inner witness of peace, and through the quiet ordering of your steps. When you emerge from the silence, you will find that He was leading you all along. The question is not whether God will speak again; the question is whether you will keep trusting, obeying, and worshiping until He does.

PRAYER

Father in the name of Jesus, grant me and every reader the grace to trust You with all our hearts; not to lean on our own understanding but to acknowledge You in all our ways, that You may direct our paths. In Jesus' name. Amen.
Proverbs 3:5-6

CONCLUSION

God Is Speaking — Are You Listening?

Throughout this book, we have explored the many ways in which God speaks — through His Word, His Spirit, His messengers, dreams, visions, circumstances, spiritual impressions, and more. We have examined how to discern His voice, how to interpret divine communication, and how to align with His perfect will. We have also seen that even in silence, God is still at work, guiding, testing, and shaping us for His glory.

The central truth is this: God desires to be heard. From the beginning, He created man for fellowship. His voice walked in the garden calling out, "Adam, where are you?" (Genesis 3:9). That same voice continues to call out to us today — not as a distant deity, but as a loving Father seeking relationship, partnership, and alignment with His divine purpose.

Yet, **as Job 33:14 declares,** *"For God may speak in one way, or in another, yet man does not perceive it."* Many have missed divine direction, breakthroughs, and destiny moments — not because God was silent, but because they did not recognize His voice or respond to His leading.

This book has equipped you with understanding, but understanding alone is not enough. It must be

coupled with pursuit. The voice of God is best heard in the context of relationship, reverence, and surrender. As you cultivate intimacy with God—through prayer, worship, the Word, and fellowship—you will sharpen your ability to hear and obey.

Let These Final Truths Guide You:

1. **God is always speaking.** He is not distant or detached; He is actively communicating His will and purpose to His children.
2. **You can hear Him.** Jesus declared, *"My sheep hear My voice…"* (John 10:27). Hearing God is not reserved for prophets or apostles—it is the inheritance of every believer.
3. **God's Word is the foundation.** Every dream, vision, or impression must align with the unchanging truth of Scripture. His Word is the plumb line for all divine communication.
4. **God speaks progressively.** He may not reveal everything at once, but He will guide you step by step as you walk in faith and obedience.
5. **His will is good, acceptable, and perfect.** Even when it is challenging, His plans for you are always redemptive, always glorious, and always for your good (Romans 12:2; Jeremiah 29:11).

A Final Call to Action

It is now your responsibility to **tune in, lean in, and walk in obedience.** God does not speak to entertain;

He speaks to direct, transform, and empower. Every word from Him carries life, wisdom, and power. Hearing God is not optional—it is essential for victorious living.

As you step into the next chapter of your life, **determine to be one who hears God clearly, responds quickly, and walks boldly** in His divine direction. Let every decision, every step, every relationship, and every assignment be filtered through His voice.

Your future is not hidden—it is only awaiting divine direction. And that direction is already available through the voice of your Father.

Prayer of Commitment

Father, in the name of Jesus, I surrender my ears, my heart, and my will to You. I declare that I will no longer walk in confusion, distraction, or doubt. Let the voice of the stranger be silenced in my life. Teach me to recognize Your voice in every season and through every circumstance. Guide me by Your Word and Spirit into the fullness of Your purpose. I declare that from this day, I walk in divine direction, supernatural insight, and the wisdom of heaven. I hear You, I trust You, and I will follow You—all the days of my life. In Jesus' name, Amen.

Final Encouragement

You were created to hear God. Let that truth settle deep in your spirit. No matter where you are in your journey — whether you are just beginning or seeking to sharpen your discernment — God is with you. He is for you. And He is speaking.

Now is the time to listen, to respond, and to walk boldly in the voice of your Father. The world is waiting for those who know His voice. Will you be one of them?

Let the journey continue.

If you will like to give your life to Jesus and be born again pray this prayer with all your heart

Altar Call
Lord Jesus, I am a sinner, and I need you to save me. I believe you died for me and rose on the third day that I may be justified. Today I confess and repent of all my sins; I forsake them; forgive me Lord Jesus; come into my heart Lord Jesus; be my Lord and savior; from today I promise to serve you in the name of Jesus.

If you prayed this prayer with all your heart, we believe you are born again. Please look for a bible Believing church and be planted or contact us at shilohttop@gmail.com

Made in the USA
Middletown, DE
23 November 2025

21515655R00109